"I read this through in one sitting—it is realistic, challenging and wonderfully helpful. I am anxious to get this book into the hands of my congregation."

ALISTAIR BEGG, Founder of *Truth for Life*

"If we are honest, none of us find evangelism easy and we make a lot of excuses. This down-to-earth, practical book provides us with useful tools to help us overcome our fear."

STEVE CLIFFORD, General Director of the Evangelical Alliance, UK

"Rico Tice has a love and passion for sharing the message of a life-changing relationship with Jesus Christ."

NICKY GUMBEL, Vicar of Holy Trinity Brompton, London; pioneer of Alpha

"Honest to a fault and deeply challenging—but big-hearted, Christ-centred and wonderfully encouraging. That is *Honest Evangelism*, because that is Rico Tice—witness to sinners and equipper of saints. *Honest Evangelism* is a much needed book from someone who knows what he is talking about."

SINCLAIR FERGUSON, Teaching Fellow of Ligonier Ministries

"A great read that is both realistic and hopeful about our evangelism, written by a man whom God has used mightily to spread the gospel. Every Christian will benefit from this."

REBECCA MANLEY PIPPERT, author of *Out of the Saltshaker* and *Uncovering the Life of Jesus*; founder of *Becky Pippert Ministries*

"A good and timely book that is rich in wisdom, grace and guidance. Challenging, liberating and above all encouraging. Read it!"

J. JOHN, Director of the Philo Trust; author of *Just10*

"We desperately need to read this book. It is compelling, and made me want to speak to my neighbours and friends about the Lord Jesus. Honest Evangelism is the Know and Tell the Gospel for today. I pray that every Christian will read it!"

GARY MILLAR, Principal, Queensland Theological College, Australia; author of *Saving Eutychus*

"There are plenty of 'how to' books on evangelism—this isn't one of them. It speaks to the heart, engages with the realities of a hardening culture, and with genuine freshness faces me with my hurts and fears and encourages me to overcome them."

HUGH PALMER, Rector of All Souls Langham Place, London

"Rico is one of the clearest and most faithful evangelists alive today, and no one is in a better position to write a book like this for cultures where the good news sounds remote and increasingly encounters hostility. I can't wait to use it."

MICHAEL HORTON, Professor of Theology and Apologetics, Westminster Seminary, California; author of *Ordinary*

"Rico Tice writes from the Christian trenches to give us a book that is realistic about witnessing, gives us reasons to keep at it, and offers us the resources to use. This book will help the church stop copying, and start helping, the world."

SIMON MANCHESTER, Rector of St Thomas, North Sydney, Australia

"I couldn't be more excited about this hard-hitting, honest book. Not only did I enjoy Tice's insights into Scripture and solid theology, I also found myself drawn to his appropriate and vivid stories throughout the book. Bottom line: I really, really like *Honest Evangelism* and commend it to you."

J. MACK STILES, Elder in the Redeemer Church of Dubai; author of *Marks of the Messenger* and *Evangelism*

RICO TICE

WITH CARL LAFERTON

Honest

EVANGELISM

How to talk about Jesus even when it's tough

For my wife, Lucy, valiant for truth
and for my father, Trevor, always providing

Honest Evangelism: *How to talk about Jesus even when it's tough*
© Rico Tice/The Good Book Company, 2015.
Reprinted 2015, 2016, 2017, 2018 (twice), 2019.

Published by:
The Good Book Company

thegoodbook.com | www.thegoodbook.co.uk
thegoodbook.com.au | thegoodbook.co.nz | thegoodbook.co.in

ISBN: 9781909919396 | Printed in India

Cover design by ninefootone creative
Design and art direction by André Parker

CONTENTS

FOREWORD

by D.A. CARSON, Professor of New Testament,
Trinity Evangelical Divinity School, Wheaton;
President of The Gospel Coalition

The changes taking place in Western cultures are both discouraging to Christians and, ironically, encouraging. More precisely, most of the changes themselves are discouraging, but they are calling forth a different set of changes that are encouraging. The book you are holding in your hand is one of these encouraging changes.

The discouraging changes are easy to list. Rising biblical illiteracy means that there is less and less cultural consensus around things like the Ten Commandments. Honour is an old-fashioned word, easily mocked; truth is increasingly flexible; the lust for power, success, and money has become more and more transparent and unchecked; dignity is old-fashioned; cruelty and vengeance are sometimes depicted as virtues.

Thirty years ago, if I were speaking with an atheist, that atheist would most likely be a "Christian" atheist; that is, the God in which the atheist did not believe would be the Christian God—which meant that the categories for discussion were still on my turf. That can no longer be assumed, and so even our efforts at evangelism are troubled by the fact that Christians live in a different world that seems alien to many people all around us.

Not long ago, I was talking with a grieving man who had recently lost his adult daughter. I commiserated with him, and slowly began to talk about life after death, and of knowing someone who had passed that way. He immediately brightened up and responded: "I know just what you mean! My daughter had a lovely garden. I think she'd like to come back as a butterfly", and once again I was struck by the brutal fact that in our respective "speeches", he and I were passing like ships in the night, living in parallel universes, needing to start much farther back if we were really going to communicate. More broadly, Christians are increasingly dismissed as intellectually inferior, or, worse yet, narrow and blind, with the presumption to insist that this Jesus of theirs is the only way to God. Christians are hate-filled bigots who should be ignored, and, perhaps, suppressed.

So where are the encouraging elements?

As the social cost of claiming to be a Christian increases, the percentage of nominal Christians decreases. To put this another way, the decline in church numbers over the past quarter-century is largely a decline in nominal believers— and that means the percentage of Christians who are in for the long haul, regardless of whether they are lauded in the culture at large, is gently increasing. Many churches that gladly affirm and preach the gospel, and that insist that genuine Christians learn to take up their cross daily, are made up of converted men and women who, with joy, delight in being forgiven by the God who made them and who will be their final Judge. These believers live their lives here with at least one eye captured by visions of eternity; that is where their greatest treasures are being stored up. In other words, at the very moment when many voices in Western cultures are turning away from the Christian foundations that played a significant role in making us what we are, a new and younger generation is turning back to the Bible again. These "encouraging elements", as I've called them, are small; but, like the cloud the size of a man's hand on the horizon in Elijah's day, they may herald mighty showers.

When the surrounding cultures become as negative toward faithful Christianity as they are, we must not forget that we are not the first generation to face such challenges. In his day, Jesus asserted that it was precisely because he spoke the truth that many did not believe (John 8 v 45). There are times when the truth is so out of phase with popular beliefs that it becomes positively repulsive to many people. When that happens, the proclamation of the truth has the effect of blinding eyes, deafening ears, and hardening hearts, as Isaiah found out (Isaiah 6 v 8-10). It is what brought Jesus to the cross. Yet ironically, it is precisely by the foolishness of Christians proclaiming the truth anyway that some hearers do repent, believe, and are saved. Or, to resort to one of Paul's metaphors, Christians and their message become a sweet, life-giving aroma to some, and the stench of death to others (2 Corinthians 2 v 15-16). In a word, biblical Christianity becomes polarising.

Rico Tice understands these things, and wants other Christians to understand them, too. In a polarised culture where Christian convictions are not in good odour, where are courage and joy in Christian witness to be found? What does Christian witness look like—both in the hard times when the mockery becomes savage, and in the good times when people are transformed by the gospel? This book, more than others in this genre, tells it like it is, and thus prepares believers to be faithful followers of Jesus, in the long train of prophets who faced ridicule long before we did (Matthew 5 v 10-12). This book thus stands as one of the encouraging markers of our day, a book that doesn't minimise the challenges, but directs us to Christ and his gospel to teach us to be overcomers.

D.A. Carson

INTRODUCTION

I find evangelism hard.

The problem with being an evangelist is that people assume that you find evangelism effortless; but I don't find it easy, and never have. For me, telling people about Jesus has often been nerve wracking. But it has been joyful. My hope in writing this book is that I'll help you experience some of the heavenly joy in finding the lost that floods out at the end of one of Jesus' most famous parables, about the shepherd who finds a lost sheep:

> *When he finds it, he joyfully puts it on his shoulders*
> *and goes home. Then he calls his friends and neighbours*
> *together and says, "Rejoice with me; I have found my*
> *lost sheep." I tell you that in the same way there will be*
> *more rejoicing in heaven over one sinner who repents*
> *than over ninety-nine righteous people who do not need*
> *to repent.*   *(Luke 15 v 5-7)*

In a few brushstrokes, Jesus shows us that something of great value is lost. There's an all-out search to find it. Then when it's found, there's unbridled joy right across heaven.

And that "something" is people. God is the great evangelist, the great seeker and finder of people; and he's called his followers to the same pursuit and the same emotion.

I've felt some of that soaring joy over the years, as I've seen the Lord seek and find lost people; and I will try and keep that before you and share it with you, while taking an honest look at some of the gruelling aspects of the loss and the search.

1. TWO HALVES OF THE STORY

Coming to Christ is such an indescribable joy.

When I was sixteen, my uncle was killed in a cliff fall. That was the first time I saw my father cry. And like dad, I had no answer to his death. So to hear from a teacher that Jesus Christ had got through death himself—and that he could get me through too—gave me such relief and hope. Suddenly, I could think of my own death and be at peace. And suddenly, life also made much more sense.

To know Jesus' love changed everything, because his love was so different from that of the world around me. I went to a school that, not surprisingly, raised its pupils on conditional love: *We'll love you if you prove yourself... if you're good enough... if you succeed.* The DNA of the whole place was about earning approval. And that kind of academic success was elusive for me, a dyslexic who couldn't read until I was nine (though on the plus side, I was very good at colouring in).

In this environment that says you aren't good enough, and so you need to prove yourself, can you imagine the joy that came in discovering that I didn't have to prove myself to God; that I was given Christ's perfection for free; that I lived by his performance and not my own?

Prove yourself—not to him.

You aren't good enough—exactly.

Succeed—he already has.

So telling other people about Jesus seemed an obvious thing to do. But very quickly, I began to be mocked for it. Sometimes there was real hatred. Some of my classmates issued a four-page spoof newsletter targeted at me. Here's a taste from the first edition:

> *"My form of Christianity," muses Rico, "consists of making myself look like a total idiot [in reality, they used a stronger word] in front of large, intelligent audiences."*
>
> *Rico, Christianity, you will find, is just a phase you're going through—don't let other people get caught up in your whirlpool of religious fantasy. Praise the Lord? Alleluyah? No. Just get lost [in reality, they used a stronger phrase].*

I'd walk into lunch with the butterflies of knowing another newsletter had been sent round. It was horrible. I remember kneeling down by my bed one day and crying. I couldn't believe this was how it had worked out. I had come to faith in Jesus and thought: *This is wonderful.* I'd told other people and they had said: "No, it's not wonderful at all".

The novelist Graham Greene once wrote: "There's always one moment in childhood when the door opens and lets the future in". This was that moment for me, and

I remember thinking: *This is only the beginning. This is what it will be like to be a Christian. But how can you go back, now you've tasted the joy of knowing Jesus?*

The painline

Why am I telling you about the schoolboy experiences of a teenager a couple of decades ago? Because I think being a Christian in the west right now, in our culture, is not dissimilar to what I experienced back then. There may not be persecution, but we're in a culture of growing hostility to Christianity. It's not just apathy we face—it's antipathy.

Many people really don't like the gospel. Sometimes they express that politely, sometimes not politely at all; but they don't like it.

This shouldn't really surprise us. Think how incendiary much of what we believe is. We believe Jesus is the only way to know God. We believe the cross is the only way to be forgiven. We believe that one day, everyone will be judged.

So if you are going to talk to people about Jesus, you are going to get hurt. It is going to sever some relationships. It is going to provoke people. Not every time, and depending on our circumstances, friendship groups, workplaces and so on, our experiences will vary; but we will face rejection enough of the time to give us second thoughts, because I don't know about you, but I don't particularly like getting hurt. We're wired to assume that if we're getting hit, something's gone wrong. And so whenever I tell someone the gospel message, and get hit (metaphorically speaking), there's a temptation either to stop saying anything, or to change what I'm saying.

I know there's a painline that needs to be crossed if I tell someone the gospel; but I want to stay the comfortable side of the painline. Of course I do!

I think that's the main reason why we don't do evangelism. Most Christians, when they first come to faith, want to tell others. Why wouldn't you?! It's brilliant—in Jesus you're in relationship with the living God; you have an answer to death; you have an answer to your sin; you have a point and a purpose to your life. But sooner or later—and in the west, it's happening increasingly soon—someone mocks you or wounds you or dislikes you. And because you're not stupid, you figure it out: *I don't want to get hit, and this keeps getting me hit, so something's gone wrong here. I'll stop doing this.*

Jesus' sheep

But Jesus himself said that this is just normal. When he sent his disciples out on their own for the first time to tell others about him, here's how he described their mission:

> *I am sending you out like sheep among wolves.*
> *(Matthew 10 v 16)*

That's what Jesus says is going on when a Christian in the workplace or the coffee shop or at the meal table opens their mouth to talk about who Jesus is, why he came and what that means. Sheep among wolves... think about that for a moment. You don't see pictures of this in children's Bibles. We don't like to think or talk about it much. But it's the image Jesus uses.

Now why is it like that? Why is telling people about

Christ so hard? Because of what our world is like. Jesus describes it so vividly in this parable:

> *A man planted a vineyard. He put a wall round it, dug a pit for the winepress and built a watchtower. Then he rented the vineyard to some farmers and moved to another place. At harvest time he sent a servant to the tenants to collect from them some of the fruit of the vineyard. But they seized him, beat him and sent him away empty-handed. Then he sent another servant to them; they struck this man on the head and treated him shamefully. He sent still another, and that one they killed. He sent many others; some of them they beat, others they killed.*　(Mark 12 v 1-5)

Jesus is aiming his words at the religious leaders of his day, but we share the same DNA as them. In other words, the picture of the vineyard is a picture of the world, and people are like God's tenants... and the tenants want to be the owners. Jesus says human beings use their freedom to deny the owner of this world his rights. We are tenants who want to be owners; so we act as if we are the owners, and we hate the real Owner. And so the Owner's messengers are not welcome. They get hit; they get hurt; they get killed.

Sheep among wolves. Messengers going to tenants who want to be owners. That's what evangelism is. That's what I realised as I knelt by my bed that night; and if you've been trying to tell friends and family about Christ, that's what you'll have discovered, too. And I bet that if you have stopped trying, it's because you've come to one of two conclusions. Either you don't think it's working, because you got hit; or you don't think it's worth it, because you got hit.

Answering when attacked

And yet the Bible tells us that, even though there are times when it hurts, we are all to be witnesses. Here's a verse that every book on evangelism quotes, so I thought this one should too:

> *In your hearts revere Christ as Lord. Always be prepared to give an answer to everyone who asks you to give the reason for the hope that you have.*   *(1 Peter 3 v 15)*

This looks great! I live with Jesus as my King, and I get ready for people to say to me: "What's different about you? I want to have what you've got. Please tell me about your hope, and where it comes from." So we sit down, I tell them the gospel, and they come to Christ and thank me for living with Christ as Lord and telling them about him.

But that's not what 1 Peter is about at all. Every chapter of that book is about how Christians suffer for being Christians. It's a letter written to churches who "suffer grief in all kinds of trials" as they're subject to "the ignorant talk of foolish people"—who face a "fiery ordeal" day by day (1 v 6; 2 v 15; 4 v 12).

So the next verse, after Peter talks of being prepared to give an answer, mentions people who "speak maliciously against your good behaviour in Christ" (3 v 16). The previous verse talks about how these Christians will "suffer for what is right" (v 14). Peter is talking about us being ready and willing to talk about our gospel hope when people are attacking us for what we believe. He's talking about being willing to cross the painline and risk getting hurt for speaking out. He's talking about being prepared to answer people when they say: "The way you live offends me, and your beliefs seem ridiculous to me" or: "I don't like Christianity. Why on earth would you believe these things?" 1 Peter 3 v 15 is about getting attacked, and then answering back clearly, about Christ, and with respect.

You will get hit

Here's the thing: Jesus says we're sheep among wolves. The Bible tells us to answer those who attack us. But most books I've read on evangelism don't tell you that. There's always this suggestion that if you do evangelism in a certain way, or if you learn to be charming or funny or interesting as you share the gospel, you can avoid getting hit.

I want to be honest: if you tell non-Christians about Jesus, it will be painful. That's what the books (other than the Bible) don't tend to tell you.

And it's because we don't have this truth firmly in place that, when we screw up the courage to tell someone about Jesus and find ourselves being rejected, we stop what we're doing or we change what we're saying. No one ever warned us that this is what evangelism can be like! So the reason I've written this book, and the reason I'm talking about hostility to the gospel as well as the joy of the gospel in this opening chapter, is just to be very honest. If you live in the west, you live in a culture that is increasingly hostile to

Christianity. That's just how it is. In the UK, I think we're pretty much at the point where to hold Christian values and to speak Christian truth is to get hated. In the US, it seems that that's where it's heading.

And elsewhere in the world, it's far, far worse. The level of persecution we risk when we talk about Christ is nothing compared to what our brothers and sisters round the world face simply for following Christ. A couple of years ago I visited the Delhi Bible Institute in India. The students at this new college are being trained to take the message of Christ Jesus to areas where people have never heard it before. These guys keep a bag, ready packed, by the back door. That's so that if people come in the front to kill them, they can grab it and run. I was talking to one of the staff there about the possibility of suffering and she said: "Of course there'll be suffering. What do you expect?" And the first graduate of the Delhi Bible Institute got martyred within six weeks. He graduated, went up into the villages, preached about Christ, and got murdered. It wasn't unexpected, and he did it anyway.

That puts the pain of rejection or mockery as a result of talking about Jesus in the west into perspective, doesn't it? Compared with what Christians face in most of the world, someone laughing or sneering at me, or turning their back on a friendship with me, is a mere pinprick of pain. And compared to what Christians will enjoy in the world to come—a perfect eternity with the Lord Jesus—the costs of evangelism are, as the apostle Paul put it, "light and momentary troubles" because there is "an eternal glory that far outweighs them all" (2 Corinthians 4 v 17).

I know that. But it doesn't feel like that. It feels more painful than a pinprick, more hurtful than something light and momentary.

The other half of the story

But all this is only half of the story. I wanted to put it first because it's the half that usually gets hidden or missed out altogether. Evangelism does hurt. You do risk your reputation and relationships if you're going to talk about Jesus. There is increasing hostility to the gospel message.

But something else is going on, too. There is also increased hunger. The same rising tide of secularism and materialism that rejects truth claims and is offended by absolute moral standards is proving to be an empty and hollow way to live.

And that means that, excitingly, you're more and more likely to find people quietly hungering for the content of the gospel, even as our culture teaches them to be hostile towards it.

To some extent, it's always been this way. In fact, it's what Paul discovered in Corinth. It's easy to think of Paul as rampaging unstoppably around the eastern Mediterranean, confidently proclaiming Christ, joyfully accepting the beatings, knowing that his message was unstoppable, that his apostleship gave him huge authority, and that churches would spring up wherever he visited.

But that's not how Paul saw his work at all. When he visited Corinth, he was visiting a city built on trade, with a culture that prized chasing experience and promoting religious pluralism. In other words, when he visited Corinth, he was visiting somewhere not unlike the places where you and I live.

He was there on mission, to evangelise. How did he feel about that?

> *I came to you in weakness with great fear and*
> *trembling. My message and my preaching were not with*
> *wise and persuasive words.*   *(1 Corinthians 2 v 3-4)*

If you've ever tried to talk about Jesus and felt weak, scared, with legs made out of jelly, and a message that sticks in your mouth and sounds halting as it leaves your lips, then you're in good company—that's exactly what Paul experienced.

It would have been the easiest thing in the world for Paul not to cross the painline. Not to stand up and talk about Jesus. Not to take the risk of rejection and mockery. But instead:

> *I resolved to know nothing while I was with you except*
> *Jesus Christ and him crucified. (v 2)*

He crossed the painline. He talked about Jesus. And... a church began. The people Paul is writing to are people who proved hungry for his message, not hostile towards it.

Paul knew that his words were insufficient. What made the difference was that they came "with a demonstration of the Spirit's power" (v 4). The Spirit had worked as he spoke. But Paul also knew that his words were necessary. It was as he "proclaimed to [them] the testimony about God" (v 1) that God worked through his Spirit and people became Christians, even as Paul was abused and rejected (Acts 18 v 5-11). Paul was a sheep among wolves; and wonderfully and miraculously, God used him to turn some wolves into sheep.

If Paul had decided not to cross the painline, he would never have seen that hunger; he would never have known the joy of seeing people become his brothers and sisters in Christ; and he could never have written several years later to a young church in that city.

Hunger: the unseen reality

Until you cross the painline, you don't know what response you will meet with. Sometimes you will get hit, just as Paul did. Sometimes you will find hunger, just as Paul did. That's been my experience. I was hit, and hit hard, at my school. Witnessing hurt. Yet at the same time, God was at work. There was hunger amid the hostility—even if I couldn't see it at the time. My schoolboy evangelistic efforts were not very smooth, or sensitive; and yet God used them. You've heard my experience of becoming a Christian at school; here's how one of my contemporaries, Richard, remembers it:

> *I knew Rico at school, though not well—we were*
> *in different classes, though we played in the same*
> *cricket team. And I distinctly remember Rico's*
> *conversion at school. I suspect if you asked most of*
> *our contemporaries, they too would remember it*
> *even though it was over 30 years ago. Why was it so*
> *memorable? For two reasons. Firstly the merciless*
> *reaction shown towards Rico—the constant, public*

and private attempts to humiliate him and get him to relinquish his new-found faith, which went on for many, many months.

Secondly, what really stuck with me was how Rico carried himself during such a difficult time for him. The easy option would have been to turn back or keep quiet but Rico stuck to his faith, and kept talking about his faith. Although I didn't realise this at the time, Rico's conversion and resolute faith sowed the first seed in my mind—who was it that gave Rico the strength to continue down such a difficult path (he surely could not have done this on his own). That was the first stage in my own journey, which many years later led me to Jesus.

When I finally accepted Jesus into my life, one of the first things I felt I needed to do was to write to Rico, despite not having been in contact for over 10 years, to let him know how his journey and struggle at school had helped me on my way.

When Richard wrote that letter to me, I cried. Back at school, I had had no idea that God was working in that way in Richard's heart. Neither did he! But stories like his remind me that for all the hostility there is to Christ, there is also a hunger for him in the hearts of those we live among. We must be honest about the hostility, or we'll have wrong expectations and give up on evangelism. But we must also be excited about the hunger, or we'll have no expectations at all, and never start evangelism.

Hostility and hunger: that's what you'll find as you tell

others about Jesus. And, of course, at the moment you open your mouth, you don't know which you're going to be met with; and you don't know what your words may do in people years later. You have to risk the hostility to discover the hunger.

But still, why is it worth the risk to your relationships and reputation? Why go through all that "fear and trembling", as Paul did? Why talk about Jesus when it's so often so tough? That's what the next chapter is about.

2. IS IT WORTH IT?

When it comes to evangelism, it can often seem the choice is like when the dentist tells you it's time for a check-up. You either make your excuses and put it off—I once avoided going for seven years—or you grit your teeth, get on with it and get it over with—which is what I do now.

But there's another way to think about evangelism, where we talk to people about Jesus because we want to, long to, and are excited to, even though it's tough.

In the second half of this book (from chapter 5 on), we'll be thinking practically about evangelism: what to say, how to be ourselves, how to get going. But of course, unless we want to do it, none of those chapters will matter very much.

So here are three truths that have helped motivate me over the years when it comes to evangelism. My prayer is that our hearts will be stirred by them, and that by having them in place, we will *want* to witness because we will know that it is *always* worth it; that "knowledge of the truth ... leads to godliness" (Titus 1 v 1).

Here they are:

1. The glory of Jesus
2. The guarantee of the new creation
3. The grim reality of death and hell

The glory of Jesus

Glory. It's a religious-sounding word, and I make no apology for using it. When it comes to Jesus, no other word will do. The glory of something is its weight, its unique worth. It's what sets something apart in an inimitable way. The glory of a sunset is its colour; the glory of a lion is its strength; the glory of a master craftsman is his skill. And in Jesus we see the nature and presence of God flood out.

God's glory is almost too much to take in. When Peter, James and John caught a glimpse of it as Jesus was transfigured in blazing white on a mountaintop, Peter spluttered rubbish—he was so "frightened" (Mark 9 v 6). When John saw the risen Jesus in his glory on Patmos, he says: "I fell at his feet as though dead" (Revelation 1 v 17). This is the glory of God, seen in Jesus; and Jesus himself said it was displayed most clearly of all, not on the mountaintop or in John's vision, but at the cross (John 12 v 23-24).

And what is our response to be to this glory? We pray for it each time we pray the Lord's Prayer: "Hallowed be your name" (Luke 11 v 2). Has it ever occurred to you that this is the number one motivation for evangelism in the Bible? The prayer here is about a concern for the honour of the Lord Jesus' name. We're asking that the Lord be treated appropriately—that at his name, every knee would

bow and every tongue confess that he is Lord. So Paul
describes his evangelistic mission, at the start of his letter
to the Romans, as calling "all the Gentiles to the obedience
that comes from faith for his name's sake" (Romans 1
v 5). Ordinary Christians in the early church "went out" to
evangelise "for the sake of the Name" (3 John v 7).

This is all about Jesus being treated in a way that
recognises his glory. Jesus himself tells us how he should
be treated in the world he has made. He is its creator, and
therefore he has authority over it. His last words to his
disciples are:

> *All authority in heaven and on earth has been given to*
> *me. Therefore go and make disciples of all nations.*
> *(Matthew 28 v 18-19)*

The theologian and statesman Abraham Kuyper put it like
this: "There is not a square inch in the whole domain of
our human existence over which Christ, who is Sovereign
over all, does not cry, 'Mine!'" Here is our mandate for
worldwide evangelism. We need permission from no
one else. The four "alls" are quite overwhelming in their
breadth:

> **All** *authority in heaven and on earth has been given to*
> *me.*
> *Go therefore and make disciples of* **all** *nations ...*
> *Teaching them to observe* **all** *that I have commanded you.*
> *And behold, I am with you* **al***ways.*   *(v 18-20, ESV)*

But the glory of Jesus is not just in his power and authority,
supreme as those are. To hallow his name is to be

overwhelmed by the sweetness of his sacrifice. He "came to them" in Matthew 28 v 18 after he'd risen from the dead, with the nail marks from his cross still fresh in his skin. He sits on the throne as the crucified one: as Revelation puts it, as "a Lamb, looking as if it had been slain" (5 v 6). And at this point it gets very, very personal because every Christian knows that the Lamb was slain for us, for each one of us:

> *He was pierced   for our transgressions,*
> *he was crushed   for our iniquities;*
> *the punishment   that brought us peace*
> *was on him,*
> *and by his wounds   we are healed.*
>   *(Isaiah 53 v 5)*

Can you see what the one with all authority was doing for *you*? Can you see how he loved you? He was *dying* for you. And the only response to the one with all power being crushed in our place is to echo the chorus of the hymn we sing each Christmas: *O come, let us adore him.*

The grief of un-adoration

So it should grieve us when Jesus is not adored, not worshipped, when his glory is not acknowledged—when he is ignored, sidelined and derided. It should grieve us when that happens in our hearts and lives; and when it happens in the hearts and lives of those around us.

In 2011, I went to St Paul's Cathedral in London for the memorial service of the Christian leader John Stott, with whom I served at All Soul's Langham Place. My most striking memory from the service was hearing his secretary of fifty-five years, Frances Whitehead, commend him to us. She said of him: "The closer I got to him, the more integrity I saw." And so her concern was that we held him in the right esteem, because she knew his character deserved it.

John Stott was a great man, but he was a mere man. How much more esteem, glory and worship does the God-man—the one with all authority, who came to be killed in our place and for our salvation—deserve? The closer you get to Jesus—the more you read of him in the Bible and see him at work in your life—the more glory you will see, and the more you will long for him to be treated as he deserves.

It's that longing that drove Paul's evangelism in Athens. There he was, in the city known for its advanced philosophy, democracy and intellectual capability... but what does he notice? What was on his postcard from Athens? What he saw was "that the city was full of idols" (Acts 17 v 16). And he was moved by what he saw; he was *greatly distressed* by those idols. He was stirred up; he was angered by what he saw—because while many false gods were being worshipped and praised, the living God, the Lord Jesus, was not. That's how he felt about a city that had pushed the true God out of the picture, that lived as though Jesus was not Lord.

In his book *Our Guilty Silence*, John Stott tells the story of Henry Martyn, a 19th-century missionary who died young, aged just 31, having given up a brilliant academic career to take the gospel to India and then to Persia (modern-day Iran):

[Martyn's] customary serenity was only disturbed when anybody insulted his Lord. On one occasion the sentiment was expressed [to Martyn] that "Prince Abbas Mirza had killed so many Christians that Christ from the fourth heaven took hold of Mahomet's skirt to entreat him to desist". It was a dramatic fantasy. Here was Christ kneeling before Mahommed. How would Martyn react? [Martyn wrote] "I was cut to the soul at this blasphemy." Seeing his discomfiture, his visitor asked what it was that was so offensive. Martyn replied: "I could not endure existence if Jesus were to be always thus dishonoured." His Muslim visitor was astonished and again asked why. "If anyone pluck out your eyes", he answered, "there is no saying why you feel pain; it is feeling. It is because I am one with Christ that I am thus dreadfully wounded."

Stott then writes:

I never read these words of Martyn's without being rebuked, for I do not have this passionate love for Christ's honour or feel this acute pain. Nor do I see it much (if at all) in the contemporary Church. But is not this the cause of our guilty silence?

We do not speak for Christ because we do not so love his name that we cannot bear to see him unacknowledged and unadored. If only our eyes were opened to see his glory, and if only we felt wounded by the shame of his public humiliation among men, we should not be able to remain silent. Rather would we

> *echo the apostles' words [in Acts 4 v 20]: "we cannot*
> *but speak of what we have seen and heard."*

Paul saw Jesus' glory, just as Henry Martyn did and we should; so he reacted to what he saw in Athens by telling them about the One who deserved their worship:

> *He was greatly distressed to see that the city was full of*
> *idols. So he reasoned in the synagogue with both Jews*
> *and God-fearing Greeks, as well as in the market-place*
> *day by day with those who happened to be there. A*
> *group of Epicurean and Stoic philosophers began to*
> *debate with him. Some of them asked, "What is this*
> *babbler trying to say?" Others remarked, "He seems*
> *to be advocating foreign gods." They said this because*
> *Paul was preaching the good news about Jesus and the*
> *resurrection.* (Acts 17 v 16-18)

Paul could not stay silent when Jesus was not known and worshipped. He was stirred up by the false worship around him. It motivated him to cross the painline, be derided as a babbler, and tell people that there is a God, who came to earth and died and rose and is on the throne of heaven; to declare that *that* God demands and deserves the worship of every single Athenian, every single human, every single inhabitant of your home and your community and your country.

These words will not be popular in a culture that calls for tolerance over truth, but we need to pray for the same spirit of indignation that we see in Paul in Athens and Henry Martyn in India. This needs to be personal. This needs to be emotional. When we see Jesus' name dishonoured, we need to pray against apathy. We need to pray for the heart of Paul, who was greatly distressed to see the godlessness of Athens, and so he spoke.

To move from giants to mice, one of the things I'm grateful for from that time at school was the grief that I, as a baby Christian, felt when my contemporaries at school did not just malign me but mocked Jesus. Thirty years later, I'm glad that I never really got over it. I shouldn't. Of course, we keep loving people and keep forgiving them even as they reject us and (worse) reject our Lord. But let's pray that the Lord will keep us from apathy about his name.

Hallowed be your name. How? We look to Jesus. Every day, we ask his Spirit to stir our hearts, so that as we read our Bibles we will not miss any of his glory. And then we will long for others to see that glory too, for his name's sake.

The guarantee of the new creation

Where will they be in 100 years time? That's what I'm trying to think when I meet new people. Wonderfully, when I think that for myself, I have an overwhelming sense of relief. My future is guaranteed by the resurrection of Jesus. He lived and taught and had a band of followers; he was tried in a Roman and a Jewish court, was sentenced to die, was strung up on a cross, had a spear put through his side, was taken off the cross and certified as dead... and three days later he was walking around again. And so now he says:

> *I am the Living One; I was dead, and now look, I am alive for ever and ever! And I hold the keys of death and Hades.* (Revelation 1 v 18)

The resurrection proves to us that there is a life beyond death, and that Jesus is in charge of it. Its past certainty gives us a future hope. It means that no matter how defeated I feel, I still walk in victory. Jesus has the future sewn up.

But here are the questions: Are you certain about eternity? And, perhaps more importantly, are you excited about eternity? In your mind, is the new creation wonderful? And why? If it isn't, then we won't be excited about telling other people that they can enjoy it for ever, too.

This is why we need to get Revelation 21 in place in our imaginations and our thinking. It's a vision of the future—the future of all Christians—given to the apostle John. Just read this slowly, and drink it in:

> *Then I saw "a new heaven and a new earth," for the first heaven and the first earth had passed away, and there was no longer any sea. I saw the Holy City, the new Jerusalem, coming down out of heaven from God, prepared as a bride beautifully dressed for her husband. And I heard a loud voice from the throne saying, "Look! God's dwelling-place is now among the people, and he will dwell with them. They will be his people, and God himself will be with them and be their God. "He will wipe every tear from their eyes. There will be no more death" or mourning or crying or pain, for the old order of things has passed away.*
>
> *He who was seated on the throne said, "I am making everything new!" Then he said, "Write this down, for these words are trustworthy and true."*
>
> *He said to me: "It is done. I am the Alpha and the Omega, the Beginning and the End. To the thirsty I will*

*give water without cost from the spring of the water of life.
Those who are victorious will inherit all this, and I will be
their God and they will be my children."*

(Revelation 21 v 1-7)

There will be a new heaven—that means a new sky—and a new earth. The old world in which we live will be removed. It will have served its purpose, but there will nevertheless be some continuity with that world; the word for "new", *kainos*, means "renewed" rather than "original". There is a sense here of re-creation. Eternal life is a physical, solid life in a perfect world.

And one thing missing from this world will be the "sea". To the Jews, the sea represented chaos in life, separation from loved ones, and the possibility of judgment (think back to what happened in Noah's day, when the sea covered the earth). So that's what "no longer any sea" means: no more chaos, no more concern, no more crying; no more terminal illness, no more last goodbyes, no more death; no more surging tides of evil and conflict, no more tyranny, no more genocides. No more sea.

God himself will see to it. He "will wipe every tear from their eyes" (v 4). The picture here is of the Lord God cupping your face in his hands, wiping tears from your cheeks like a doting parent, and saying: *Never again. It's all over. It's all done.*

A new city

That's the new earth. And in the new earth we see a new city, "the new Jerusalem". Jerusalem in the Old Testament was the place where God met his people. And human language proves a bit inadequate for describing how great it will be, and certainly I don't have space here to do it any kind of justice. But let me give you two themes.

First, John uses the picture of marriage—"a bride beautifully dressed for her husband" (v 2)—to describe the intimacy of the church's eternal relationship with Jesus. God is saying: *Take the best moments relationally that you've ever known, whether you knew them for years and years or just in some fleeting moments. Take those moments you never want to end, and this is what it will feel like to be with my Son Jesus, only better, and for ever.* The truth is that you haven't yet known 99.9% of the blessings of the Christian life, because they're in the world to come. If you don't believe me, let's talk again in 10,000 years time!

Second, there's complete security. Verse 12—"It had a great, high wall with twelve gates, and ... on the gates were written the names of the twelve tribes of Israel". This symbolises the safety of God's people. This is home, and nothing bad can come in to harm its inhabitants, and they will never be thrown out.

And what is it that makes this holy city in this renewed earth so perfect, peaceful, pain-free, intimate and secure?

> *Then the angel showed me the river of the water of life,*
> *as clear as crystal, flowing from the throne of God and of*
> *the Lamb. (22 v 1)*

In the middle of this city is a throne, and on the throne sit God the Father and God the Son. God is perfect. The best thing about his place is him. You'll spend an eternity getting to know him more, appreciating him more deeply, enjoying him for ever. You cannot begin to imagine how great this is—and it's your future.

And the truth is, anyone can come and enjoy it with you. In 21 v 6, Jesus says: "To the thirsty I will give water without cost from the spring of the water of life". Well, who doesn't thirst for this perfect life? Everyone is striving for it. The problem is, most people look for this "water" in the wrong places. It's only truly offered by Jesus. As he told a woman who had made a mess of her life by looking in the wrong places:

> Whoever drinks the water I give them will never thirst.
> Indeed, the water I give them will become in them a
> spring of water welling up to eternal life.   (John 4 v 14)

Jesus came to give living water, at no cost to those who accept it but at monumental cost to himself. And in the new creation, we will live in Jesus' presence and drink from the water of life, for ever. Anyone can.

So evangelism is like pointing a parched friend to the fountain. You and I have found the fountain; many around us have not. Our joyful privilege is to tell them where it is to be found, by telling them about Jesus.

So why witness? Because the new creation is wonderful and the future is certain. Maybe we should read Revelation 21 and 22 each day when we get up. If we're excited about where we're heading, or rather who we're heading towards, we'll be motivated to tell others that they can be heading there, too.

The grim reality of death and hell

One of the reasons my uncle's death was such a terrible shock to me was the fact that no one had ever spoken to me about death, either at home or at school, for the first sixteen years of my life. It just wasn't mentioned. Death is not a common or popular subject in western culture. We'd rather lie to ourselves, convincing each other that people don't die: they "fall off their perch" or "go upstairs" or "pass on" or "become a star in the sky".

The Bible, by contrast, always tells the truth; and when it speaks of our lives, it does so with the emphasis on their brevity. We're described as the morning mist, chaff being thrown into the air, flowers of the field that blow away, just a memory of a dream when you wake up and, perhaps most devastatingly of all, as a sigh and we're gone. No wonder the writer of Psalm 90 asks God to "teach us to number our days, that we may gain a heart of wisdom" (v 12).

I wonder, though, if death isn't what people don't want mentioned, so much as what comes next. And we're right to be worried, because the Bible is clear that "people are destined to die once, and after that to face judgment" (Hebrews 9 v 27)—to face the potential punishment of hell.

In the 21st century, many people either dismiss hell as a myth, or treat it as a joke. They joke that they'd rather be in hell than heaven, because all their friends will be in hell too, and it will be much more fun.

Jesus did not view hell like that. He once told a harrowing story about a rich man who died:

[He] was buried. In Hades [hell], where he was in
torment, he looked up and saw Abraham far away.

(Luke 16 v 22-23)

We need to hear Jesus telling us that hell is *real*. Let's be clear: to say there is no hell or to live as if there is no hell is to call Jesus a liar.

And Jesus tells us that hell is a place of *suffering*. There's no fun in hell. No friendship either. Hell means being totally separated from God's mercy and blessing. Everything good that we enjoy now is, whether people realise it or not, a gift from God. In hell, there are no gifts. That's God's punishment on those who choose eternity without him. The worst you have experienced in this life is only a glimmer of what it is like. As the rich man in Jesus' parable describes it, it is "agony" (v 24).

Unsurprisingly, the rich man asks for some relief from the agony. But he is told—and this is harrowing and heart-breaking:

Between us [in heaven] and you a great chasm has been
set in place, so that those who want to go from here to
you cannot, nor can anyone cross over from there to us.

(v 26)

Hell as Jesus describes it is *final*, and fixed. There are no more chances—God gives people this life to make their decision. He treats us as adults, and gives us what we've chosen—life with him, or life without him.

Finally, hell is *deserved*. Why do people go to hell? Because they reject Jesus. The essence of sin is to not believe in him (John 16 v 9). It is to suppress the truth about him (Romans 1 v 18). And Jesus is very clear that at the end of the age he will:

> ... *weed out* ... *everything that causes sin and all who do evil. [His angels] will throw them into the blazing furnace, where there will be weeping and gnashing of teeth.*   (Matthew 13 v 41-42)

Loving people means warning people

I was once in Australia visiting a friend. He took me to a beach on Botany Bay, so I decided I had to go for a swim. I was just taking off my shirt when he said: "What are you doing?" I said: "I'm going for a swim". He said: "What about those signs?" And he pointed me to some signs I'd not really noticed—*Danger: Sharks!*

With all the confidence of an Englishman abroad, I said: "Don't be ridiculous—I'll be fine". He said: "Listen mate, 200 Australians have died in shark attacks—you've got to decide whether those shark signs are there to save you or to ruin your fun. You're of age—you decide."

I decided not to go for a swim.

These words about hell are all straight from Jesus' lips. And they're a loving warning to us. The reason Jesus talked about hell is because he does not want people to go there. The reason Jesus died was so that people wouldn't have to go there. The only way to get to hell is to trample over the cross of Jesus.

That is a great motivator for our witness, too—we want to point people to Jesus, who not only warned about hell but went through hell so that no one else needs to.

It is loving to warn people about hell. Some of the most

striking words I've read about this are those of someone who isn't a Christian, but who gets the point. He's Penn Jilette, (of Penn and Teller, the magician double-act). Here's what he said about evangelism, or proselytism:

> I've always said that I don't respect people who don't proselytise. I don't respect that at all. If you believe that there's a heaven and a hell, and people could be going to hell or not getting eternal life, and you think that it's not really worth telling them this because it would make it socially awkward ... how much do you have to hate somebody to not proselytise? ... I mean, if I believed, beyond the shadow of a doubt, that a truck was coming at you, and you didn't believe that truck was bearing down on you, there is a certain point where I tackle you. And this is more important than that.

We must beware of living as functional atheists. Deep down, I know hell is real and terrible. And in church on a Sunday, I sing about the reality that Jesus is the only way it can be avoided. But Monday to Friday in the office, at home with non-Christian relatives, when visiting friends who are rejecting Jesus—I live as though it isn't true. I live as though they won't die, as though hell isn't where they're heading, and so I don't say anything. It is loving to warn an English tourist who is about to swim with sharks. It is unloving not to warn him just because you don't want to spoil his day or have him call you ridiculous.

And that's just it; it's all about love. My willingness to tell people the gospel is a test of my love for them. This couldn't have come home to me any more clearly than when I was playing rugby at university. I'd given a guy in the rugby team a tape (I'm old enough that it was a tape, not a podcast) of a sermon I'd preached. It was on John 1 v 29: "Behold, the Lamb of God, who takes away the sin of the world" (ESV). I remember that in the sermon, I simply and starkly said that either we pay for our sin in hell, or the Lamb pays for us on the cross.

This friend, called Ed, played my sermon one night to his housemates, who were in the same rugby team as us; and one of them, Dave, got very upset. He said: "If that's what Rico believes, the fact he's said nothing of it to me in months means he's not really my friend". So Ed rang me up and said: "Rico, you need to speak to Dave; he's upset that you've not talked to him till now about what's in the sermon."

And Dave was right. If I'd really loved him, I'd have warned him about hell, shown him the cross, and invited him to trust Jesus and spend eternity with him in the new creation. It was a life-changing phone call. I found myself praying that I wouldn't only have a sense of God's love for me, but that I would have that same love for others: that I would love them enough to risk rejection in order to speak to them about Jesus and warn them about hell.

Don't be deluded. Everyone needs Jesus. Everyone. We have to keep remembering that we are like grass. We may be flourishing now, but death is real. It doesn't always warn us of its arrival, and without Jesus, what lies beyond is terrible; and so everyone needs to hear about him.

So this is why we talk about Jesus, even though it is tough. This is why it is always worth it. Hell is a terrible reality we desperately want people to avoid. The new creation is a wonderful place we urgently want people to enjoy. And the Lord Jesus deserves glory, and supremely we want him to be given it. That's why we evangelise. That's what gets us being willing to—and even wanting to—take the risk of crossing the painline.

Unless...

There's one reason why we still won't evangelise.

3. WHY WE (STILL) WON'T EVANGELISE

We all have moments in life we wish we could rewind to and do things very differently. For me, the thing I most regret is what happened before my grandmother's death. Or rather, what didn't happen.

My grandmother died absolutely convinced that God would accept her because she was a good person. She had no faith in Christ. My brother and I were the only Christians in the family at that point, and my brother broke down in tears when he did the Bible reading at her funeral. I was the only one who knew why. She had died without Christ.

And here's what I regret. In the week before my grandmother died, I did not speak to her about Jesus. I loved her, but I didn't say anything to her. When my other grandmother had died, I'd taken her hand and prayed with her. But not that grandmother. I just let her go.

Why didn't I tell her about Christ? I've come to realise that I was afraid of what she'd say, and I was afraid of what my family would say, because I knew they'd think it was inappropriate and unhelpful. I was afraid.

I loved my grandmother, and she loved me, but the hard truth is that I loved myself more than her. I wanted my family to think well of me more than I wanted her to think of Christ as her Saviour. That's why I didn't speak to her. I loved myself more than I loved her and more than I loved my Lord.

And that means that my family's respect and having an easy time in life had become idols to me. There has to be something in our hearts that we make the most important thing in life, and to which we sacrifice other things to have or to keep it. If that something isn't God, then it's an idol. Idols can be good things, that God gave us to enjoy; the problem comes when we elevate them to divine status— when we love them more, and think we need them more, than him. And when it came down to it, the hard truth was that I wanted my family to respect me more than I wanted to bring Jesus glory or see my grandmother saved. It was my idol—a good thing elevated into a divine thing—and I was so afraid of losing it that I kept my mouth shut.

The divine waiter

I've often wondered why lovely, compassionate, committed Christians simply don't do evangelism. For years, I couldn't understand why so many well-taught and in many ways mature believers were just apathetic about sharing the gospel. They knew about the new creation; they believed in the reality of hell; they confessed Jesus as their King and Saviour. Some of them had even seen people come to faith through their witness in the past. But they were half-hearted at best about evangelism.

The danger of a book on evangelism (and indeed on prayer) is that people who are actually trying hard to follow Christ, who love him and are deeply grateful, just feel beaten down. I'd hate that to be the case here, but we do need to brace ourselves for some spiritual cardiology—for a diagnosis of the way in which our hearts are working, so that we can more clearly focus on Christ, which, miraculously, is what we most want deep down.

Here's what I slowly came to conclude had happened to these committed, non-evangelising Christians: in their hearts, they were serving something good that they had made into their god—their idol. And that's what was stopping them from evangelising.

The Bible is clear that everyone worships something. And naturally, we're the people Paul describes in Romans 1 v 25, who have "served created things rather than the Creator". Anything that we serve instead of God is a created thing, an idol. Money, reputation, power, career, family, and so on—these are all good things that we can turn into "god things". Our hearts get kidnapped.

When we worship an idol, we turn God into a divine waiter. He is there to deliver our daydream to us. We touch base with him on a Sunday; we put our order in via prayer; we might give a decent tip in the collection plate. But God is essentially there to give us what we feel we need—our idol. And we get furious with him if he doesn't deliver.

Becoming a Christian doesn't automatically or immediately cure us of this idol-worship. At the heart of all sin is idolatry in the heart—loving and obeying something other than our loving God. I am constantly struggling to keep the Lord Jesus at the centre of my heart, to find my identity and assurance and purpose and satisfaction in him.

And unless I do, I will not speak about him. After all, we talk about what we love. If you've ever had a friend who has just got engaged, and you've listened to them talk about their loved one non-stop for hours (or if you've ever been that person!), you'll know this is true.

So for as long as Jesus is not my greatest love, I will keep quiet about him in order to serve my greatest love, my idol. I will keep quiet about him because I am afraid of losing my greatest love, my idol. Suppressing the truth about Christ is the effect of our wicked worship of created things, and it makes God angry, says Paul:

> *The wrath of God is being revealed from heaven against*
> *all the godlessness and wickedness of people, who*
> *suppress the truth by their wickedness.* *(Romans 1 v 18)*

Idol-spotting

So if we know why we should witness and we're still not willing to witness, then it's because our hearts are somewhere else. It's because actually what we most want is a comfortable life, or a good reputation with friends and colleagues, or a nice settled existence with our family, and so on.

For me, I worshipped the approval of my family more than I worshipped my Saviour, so I kept quiet. I loved the approval of my family more than I loved my Lord or my grandmother, so I didn't witness.

We have to not just notice the idols of our city, as Paul did in Athens; we need to see the ones in our hearts.

They're what stop you witnessing. So, ask yourself:

1. What do you daydream about? Your idols are the things that, in reality, you most care about having, increasing, or keeping.

2. What do you have nightmares about? Our idols are the things that we most fear losing, that we can't imagine living without, that keep us awake at night worrying.

3. What do you pray about? If there is something we pray for more than for God's will to be done in our lives and the lives of our loved ones, it's likely that it's our functional god. If my prayer for my sons is that they'll be happy, or healthy, or married, or successful, rather than that they'll know Jesus and live for him whatever the cost, then I'm worshipping idols.

4. What do you need in life that, if you get it, means you'll then live for God? If I find myself thinking: *Yes, I'll obey you God, once I've got... [fill in the blank]* or: *Yes, I will take risks to witness about Jesus, once I've just achieved...* then the end of that sentence is my idol.

The reason that, even if we have everything straight in our heads, we won't witness is because of what's going on in our hearts. That's why we say enough to salve our consciences—we talk about church, or Jesus' love, or how great it is to pray—but we won't say enough to help people be saved: we won't talk about death, or sin, or hell, or salvation.

This is the shortest chapter in this book. But in many ways it's the most important one. I've come to see that I can have all the understanding I need, I can have a great way of explaining the gospel, I can talk the talk with other Christians, I can read (or even write) books about evangelism... but unless I have identified and am uprooting the idols of my heart, I still won't actually get across that painline and tell people about Jesus. And neither will you.

And what is the key to battling our idols? The first step is spotting them in the first place! We need the Spirit's spotlight as we cry out:

> Search me, God, and know my heart ... see if there is
> any offensive way in me.   (Psalm 139 v 23)

For years, I thought the reason why I hadn't spoken to my grandmother was a lack of love (it was), but I had no idea that the idol of family approval drove that lack of love. To see this idol for the first time was sobering and shaming; but it also meant I could move forwards.

Once you can name your idols, when you start to see them working, you can confess them, and ask others to pray for you about them, and begin to look out for them. And you can begin consciously to seek what you have been looking for from that idol in the only place where you will truly find it—the Lord Jesus. We need to replace our idols with the real God: Christ.

So if I could turn the clocks back now to my grandmother's deathbed in 1988, I would pray before I go to see her: *Lord, you know I've often found my identity in family approval. Please forgive me; thank you that my true identity is in Christ; thank you that in him I have your approval as my heavenly Father. So please help me to be unafraid of my family's rejection as I seek to speak to my grandmother. Please give me the kindness and gentleness of Jesus, and yet give me the boldness to ask to pray with her about the Lord Jesus, who is the Good Shepherd who lays down his life for the sheep.*

If we're to share Christ, we need first to love Christ! We need to ask the Spirit to go to work in our hearts with the gospel, so that we'll love Christ more and more, and he'll displace our idols; and so when we talk about what we love, we'll be talking about him.

4. WHAT MUST I REMEMBER?

Part of any pastor's job is to help people proclaim Christ in the circumstances God has placed them. To make a huge generalisation, the Christians I meet up with tend to fall into two categories. And let me quickly add that all too often, I fall into Category Two—and I'm paid to do evangelism!

Category One

Here's the person who really does see their life as defined by being one of "Christ's ambassadors" (2 Corinthians 5 v 20). They expend energy and emotion to perform this role. They pray for, look for, and take opportunities to witness. They get really excited about things like Christmas, because it's an event on everyone's lips, and carol services are the easiest invitation of the year. Their friends and colleagues don't only know they are a Christian, but they have been told about Christ—because this person has told them.

Category Two

Here's the Christian who's been a churchgoer for many years. They are a loving friend or spouse or parent. They read their Bible and pray. They know their doctrine. But as I probe, it becomes obvious that this person has a view of Christian faith that does not include Christian witness. Somehow, their view of godliness has had evangelism removed from it. Witnessing is an optional extra in the Christian life, and they've opted out. They may have colleagues they have worked alongside for years, who don't even know they're a Christian or who think that they have a hobby they do on Sundays called "church"—a little like golf, but without the fresh air.

I know what it's like to be a category two person, because many times I've found myself there. Maybe you do too. Perhaps you know that you should be evangelising. You read chapter two of this book and thought: *I want to witness.* Yet somehow, you always stay the safe side of the painline. In this chapter, I want to articulate three truths that I have seen again and again move someone (including myself) from category two into category one. If we remember these truths, we'll share our faith.

Here are the three things: God's sovereignty, God's grace, and God's power.

God's sovereignty

Here are a few verses that really transformed my evangelism.

We're rejoining Paul in Athens. Having started to witness to the risen Christ in the marketplace, he's invited to the Areopagus, the assembly of the movers and shakers in Athens. They want to "know what this new teaching is that you are presenting" (Acts 17 v 19).

So Paul goes in and he tells them the truth about God, about Christ, and about how one day he will judge, but that today his hearers can repent and be saved. As he does that, here's what he says about God and about people:

> *The God who made the world and everything in it is the Lord of heaven and earth and does not live in temples built by human hands. And he is not served by human hands, as if he needed anything. Rather, he himself gives everyone life and breath and everything else. From one man he made all the nations, that they should inhabit the whole earth: and he marked out their appointed times in history and the boundaries of their lands.*
>
> *(v 24-26)*

So there is a God who made the world and everything in it, including my neighbours, my relatives and my work colleagues. He made everything and everyone. And he doesn't need them, but they need him—he gives all of us every breath we take. Not only that, but he has marked out how long every person will live, and decided where they will live.

Now, hold onto your seat as we think about what this means. Your neighbour lives down your street because God put them there. Your colleague at work sits at the next desk to you because God sat them there.

A family recently moved into our street in London, just opposite. They're Muslims. Why have they moved in? They think it's for work, and because it's close to a mosque. But no—in fact, God has put them there. Why? Let's have a look at the next verse:

God did this so that they would seek him and perhaps reach out for him and find him, though he is not far from any one of us. (v 27)

In God's sovereignty, what is going on in history is that God is reaching out to people, so that they will reach out for him. The reason your neighbour lives where she does is so that she will get reached for the gospel. Why did God want a Christian—you—to be in your workplace? Yes, so you can bless your boss and workers by working hard and honestly. But first and foremost, it's so that others there can hear the gospel.

It's no accident that you know the people you do. It's no accident that they're in your path. They need the gospel. You know the gospel. God wants them to hear the gospel.

And that transforms how I look at my life. It makes it really exciting. If I'm sitting on a train and there's someone opposite me, God has put them there. He's not far from them, because I know him and I'm sitting opposite them. Now that transforms whether I'll bother to try to start a conversation with them. It'll transform what I aim to talk about with them. And it'll transform how I pray for my day ahead; I'll be praying for energy and love to make the most of every divine appointment that God has already written into my schedule.

We need to believe that God is in charge of which desk we sit at. We need to understand that God has put people around us because he wants them to hear the gospel. We need to grasp God's sovereignty.

God's grace

Who are you?

Fundamentally, you and I are adopted children of God. That is who a Christian is:

> *The Spirit you received does not make you slaves, so that you live in fear again; rather, the Spirit you received brought about your adoption to sonship. And by him we cry, "Abba, Father" ... we are heirs—heirs of God and co-heirs with Christ.* (Romans 8 v 15, 17)

Now this is remarkable, not least because it is utterly undeserved. We are people who find that: "I do not do the good I want to do, but the evil I do not want to do—this I keep on doing" (7 v 19). God knows who we are and what we are like, and yet he says: *I still love you and I will sort out your mess, and I will treat you like my child, like my Son, Jesus.* That is God's grace—his undeserved and lavish kindness. He takes a wretch like me and he loves me as his child.

Let me take you back to spring 2011. In the UK, it was Royal Wedding time; Prince William, second in line to the throne, was about to get married. You and I know that William had found a bride, Kate Middleton, at his university. But imagine that he'd gone about finding his wife rather differently. Imagine that the day before his wedding, he'd gone down to Soho, and gone into one of the brothels there, and found a woman who had sold herself into prostitution because she wanted the money, and who was now living in a filthy, sleazy bedsit, and he'd taken her by the hand and got down on one knee and said: *I want to marry you, and I won't take no for an answer.*

Imagine that he'd set the date, given her a choice of any wedding dress she wanted, and then when the big day arrived he had taken her to Westminster Abbey, and said: *She's my wife. She's part of the royal family now. She will inherit all that I will inherit. Treat her as what she is—royalty.*

That would, of course, never happen. *Except that it has.* It has happened to every Christian. The Bible says that we are adopted children of God, with Jesus as our Brother; and that we are the bride of God, with Jesus as our Bridegroom. He really has come and plucked us out of our dirty, sleazy, desperate sinfulness, and cleaned us up and married us and brought us into the divine royal family.

For the Christian, "there is now no condemnation for those who are in Christ Jesus" (8 v 1). Our Brother Jesus has taken all our sin and dealt with it. We have the utter security of knowing that we will not be condemned. For the Christian, "God works for the good of those who love him ... to be conformed to the image of his Son" (8 v 28-29). God is changing us, working in us to enable us to resist sin and become more and more like our Brother Jesus. And for the Christian, "our present sufferings are not worth comparing with the glory that will be revealed in us" (8 v 18). There will be a day when we are in our Father's home, in our Father's arms, and sin and suffering will be past.

The amazing truth is this: when the Creator God looks at you, he sees his child. He sees someone whom he loves, whom he is delighted with, whom he will do anything for. God has given you, and is giving you, and will give you, all that is his Son's. Today, there is nothing you can do, and nothing that can happen to you, that will separate you from God's love or stop you from getting home (v 38-39).

And this needs to be at the core of how we see ourselves. The nineteenth-century poet and novelist Victor Hugo wrote: "Life's greatest happiness is to be convinced you're loved". Well, the Christian can be utterly convinced that we are wonderfully loved by the most powerful One in the universe.

Our problem is that, often, what we know in our heads doesn't make it to our hearts. The New York pastor Tim Keller tells of how in the basement of his apartment block there used to be a coke can machine. You put your money in and made your selection, but the can didn't come out for you to enjoy unless you banged the machine all the way down, so that the can actually dropped out.

We need to do that with God's grace. We need to bang it down into our hearts, so that we don't simply understand it, but we also live and breathe it.

Now, how does grasping God's grace make a difference to you in your evangelism? It means that we know that, as the Australian evangelist John Chapman put it: "Whether you accept or reject me does not make me more or less valuable".

When we know we are children of God, we don't fear the rejection of others—we're loved by our Creator! We don't fear their mockery—the Maker of the cosmos thinks well of us! We don't fear their withholding of a favour or a promotion or anything else—we're heading to glory in heaven.

A Christian knows that in Christ we have all we need, and cannot lose any of it; and so, rather than being driven by the need for approval or love from others, we're free to love them by sharing the gospel with them.

We need to know that the opinion of our family, friends and workmates is not what gives us value. We need to believe that we are deeply loved children of God.

God's power

The problem with actually doing evangelism is that it just doesn't work. You're never successful—people don't become Christians. The other problem is that you might get it wrong. You're not good enough at it—you can't answer the questions, or you don't say it in a way that's interesting or funny or striking (or whatever) enough.

If you feel like that, you're right. Your evangelism will never make someone come to faith in Christ. And your evangelism will never be good enough to win someone.

But here's the thing; it doesn't have to be.

That's not your job. When it comes to witnessing, the most liberating truth is to realise what our job is, and what God's job is:

> *The god of this age has blinded the minds of unbelievers, so that they cannot see the light of the gospel that displays the glory of Christ, who is the image of God. For what we preach is not ourselves, but Jesus Christ as Lord, and ourselves as your servants for Jesus' sake. For God, who said, "Let light shine out of darkness," made his light shine in our hearts to give us the light of the knowledge of God's glory displayed in the face of Christ.*
> *(2 Corinthians 4 v 4-6)*

We know that the minds of unbelievers are blinded. We experience it every day. Why don't people want to know about Jesus? Why don't they think about eternity? Why, when they're told, don't they come to faith? Because "they cannot see the light of the gospel". They're blind! They just can't get it. And neither you nor I are spiritual eye surgeons. Nothing you and I do or say can give spiritual sight.

So what hope is there?

> God, who said, "Let light shine out of darkness," made
> his light shine in our hearts. (v 6)

God turns on the lights, Paul says. And when did God first say: *Turn on the light?* It was as he created the world:

> The earth was formless and empty, darkness was over the
> surface of the deep, and the Spirit of God was hovering
> over the waters. And God said, "Let there be light," and
> there was light.   *(Genesis 1 v 2-3)*

In 2 Corinthians 4 Paul is saying that if you are a Christian, God took the same power that made the world, and he used it to give us sight: to give us hearts that understand that in knowing Jesus, we know God in all his majesty, perfection and love.

That's what happened when you became a Christian. The power of God's Spirit recreated your heart so that you could see who Jesus is. It took the power necessary to make stars to do that. And God has that power. Only he can do it—but he *can* do it.

Now, if he can do it for you, he can do it for your friend or family member or work colleague. Think of the person you know who seems least likely ever to come to Christ in faith. Then think of the power that created light for the first time. Do you think God can't bring them to faith? Do you think the Spirit cannot work to recreate their hearts?

The Spirit's power should give us the confidence to cross the office or the street or the front room and tell someone about Jesus. That's what it did for Paul:

> What we preach is not ourselves, but Jesus Christ as
> Lord.   (2 Corinthians 4 v 5)

We don't talk about ourselves and point to ourselves—we preach Christ; we talk about him with others. The gospel is so powerful because it is the power of God to open blind eyes and bring faith.

We talk about Christ: *God* opens blind eyes. It is my job, and your job, to tell someone about Jesus—who he is, why he came and what it means. It is not our job to make someone respond. It's God who opens blind eyes. You communicate the message—and then you pray that he would do the miracle.

This is so liberating. What is successful witnessing? It's not someone becoming a Christian—it's someone hearing about Christ. It's not you winning the argument, having all the answers, or giving an eloquent speech—it's you preaching Christ.

Paul knew that. He knew the Spirit's power, and he knew his own role. Look at how Paul's mission-team member, Luke, recounts the conversion of one woman:

> We travelled to Philippi ... [where we found] a place of
> prayer. We sat down and began to speak to the women

> *who had gathered there. One of those listening was a*
> *woman from the city of Thyatira named Lydia, a dealer*
> *in purple cloth. She was a worshipper of God. The Lord*
> *opened her heart to respond to Paul's message. When*
> *she and the members of her household were baptised, she*
> *invited us to her home."*   *(Acts 16 v 12-15)*

What did Paul do? He gave Lydia—a non-Jew who sought to live God's way—the message. He talked about Christ. The Lord opened her heart to respond. Paul preached: God opened blind eyes. John Stott explains it like this in *The Message of Acts*:

> *Although the message was Paul's, the saving initiative*
> *was God's. Paul's preaching was not effective in itself;*
> *the Lord worked through it. And the Lord's work*
> *was not itself direct; he chose to work through Paul's*
> *preaching. It is always the same.*

Our job is not to convert people. It is to witness to Christ. Conversion isn't the mark of a successful witness— witnessing is. Think about a courtroom. Witnesses are there to tell the truth. That's successful witness. If the jury doesn't believe them, that's not their fault or their failure. You have not failed if you explain the gospel and are rejected. You have failed if you don't try.

What we must remember

Let me take you back to the two categories I began with. What will get those of us who find ourselves in category two to share the gospel with people we meet, and with those we've known for years but have never told about Jesus?

What do we need to tell ourselves as we look at someone who doesn't know Jesus, whether it's in the factory or the office, the coffee shop or sports club, or in our own home? What do we need to remember as we look at someone we know doesn't trust Jesus?

- *God is sovereign. He has put me here and he has put them here so that they can hear the gospel.*
- *God is gracious. He loves me as he loves Jesus. I'm a child of God. Their response to the gospel will not make me any more or less valuable or accepted or loved.*
- *God is powerful. His Spirit opened my blind eyes— his Spirit can open theirs. My job is to preach Christ. The rest will be up to God.*

If we get those three truths about God in place in our hearts and heads, we'll get praying, we'll start looking for chances to talk about Jesus, and if they don't come up naturally, at some point we'll take a deep breath and say: *I'd like to tell you about Jesus.* We might be feeling weak and fearful, and find ourselves trembling as we do it, just as Paul did in Corinth. It might not come out as we'd hoped. It will mean taking a risk. But if we get those three things in place, we'll cross the painline.

5. WHAT DO I SAY?

Recently, Barclays Bank produced some life skills ads, created to help young people boost their chances of getting a job. Banks aren't hugely popular right now, but Barclays did get this right. The ads highlight the importance of making eye contact, standing properly, using the right language, dressing appropriately and not saying "um" before every sentence.

You can be the brightest, most hard-working and committed potential worker in the world; but if you don't have those kinds of "life skills", you're likely to stay a potential worker, rather than an actual one!

And the truth is that when it comes to evangelism, while of course you need to be committed to doing it, you also need to be able to do it. What are the life skills required for evangelism? One, of course, is knowing what to say; and that's what this chapter is mainly about. But moving straight to what to say is jumping a crucial stage—because for many, the problem is not that they don't want to do it, or don't know what to say, but that they never seem to get an opportunity to evangelise. Christianity just never crops up when they talk to people. So before we turn to what to say, the question is: how do you get to a conversation about the gospel?

Being and doing in order to be saying

When God said: "Let us make mankind in our image" (Genesis 1 v 26), he was saying something crucial about every single person you know. The people we interact with each day are the pinnacle of God's creation. They are designed by God in his image—to work, to relate, to be creative, to shape the world around them, and so on. Of course, that's not everything that can be said about humanity being made in God's image—but it does mean that we can and should celebrate people and their passions, enjoying the way they reflect God's image.

So on my street, there's a guy who loves motor-racing, another who is into gardening, a third who is an international rowing referee... and I want to have a genuine interest in what they're interested in. I want to enjoy them, because they are people made in God's image, never "projects" for my evangelism. Put simply, I'm only going to be effective in witnessing if I'm being someone who is actually interested in them as people.

Essential to this is the ability to ask questions. It was said of John Chapman that he was interested in everything. That meant that questions just poured out of him because he found life, people, culture and the world fascinating. He loved people, and so he asked questions. We need to listen to people more than we speak to them; and that means asking questions. After all, if you want people to ask you questions about what makes you tick, then you need to ask them questions about what makes them tick. Don't just wait for someone to ask you about Christianity and wonder why they never do. Ask questions; and then make sure you listen to the answers! We need to be being that kind of interested, engaged person.

Next, we need to be people who are engaged in the "doing" of Christianity. We need to show the gospel if we're to have a chance to share the gospel. Jesus tells us to:

> Let your light shine before others, that they may see your good deeds and glorify your Father in heaven.
>
> (Matthew 5 v 16)

So I want to do acts of kindness for the people on my street. I want to invite them into being compassionate alongside me, so they can see Christianity in action. For instance, my church has an initiative for serving the homeless, and I might ask my friends on our street to come along and help us serve those who have so little. I'd love my neighbours to see what Christians do. This is what Peter has in mind when he says:

> Live such good lives among the pagans that, though they accuse you of doing wrong, they may see your good deeds and glorify God on the day he visits us.
>
> (1 Peter 2 v 11-12)

The sense is that people end up feeling conflicted by the Christians who live among them. They want to accuse them of doing wrong, because they want to go on rejecting the gospel rather than having to think about it, and yet, as they watch what Christians do, they are drawn to them, rather than able to criticise them.

It is really only if you and I being this kind of person, and doing these kind of things, that we'll begin to be able to start saying what we want to. And that begins in two ways: chatting our faith, and asking "pain-line questions".

By chatting our faith, what I mean is that we need to make Christianity an everyday, natural part of our conversations with people. Knowing Jesus is an integral, important part of your life, so it can and should be part of what you chat about; not always in formal, "now-I-am-sharing-the-gospel-with-you" ways, but as part of conversations about what we did at the weekend, how we're dealing with an issue at home or work, why we're really busy at the moment, and so on. By raising an aspect of your faith in conversation—even if that conversation then moves on to other subjects—you have shown the person you're speaking to that Christian faith is relevant to real life, that it's important to your life, and that you're open to them asking you about it. It's so easy to talk about everything but Christ. So aim to chat your faith in low-key, natural, conversational ways.

Second, though, I have discovered that I need to come up with a "pain-line question" for people I want to talk to about Christ. This is a question that draws on the relationship I have with someone and the circumstances I know they are in and the interests I know they have. It's a question designed to move a conversation into an area where I might be able to start talking about the gospel. It's a question that comes with a risk, because it might meet with hostility.

So for instance, for my friend who is young and suffers with chronic neck pain, I want gently to ask her: "What if your neck never gets better?" I'm hoping for a chat about the difference between human happiness—which depends on all our circumstances being "good"—and Christian joy—which is internal and hope-filled whatever our circumstances, because it relies on knowing Jesus and that he is for us and has saved us.

Or for my neighbour who loves gardening, I want to ask them what they think is behind the beauty of the natural world. And for my other neighbour who seems very angry with God, I want to summon up my courage and just say: "Why are you so angry with God? What has made you feel this way?"

These are pain-line questions—they get across the pain-line. When you ask a question like that, you don't know how someone will respond, but it gives the opportunity for a really natural, helpful conversation to open up, and for you to discover hunger in your friend—and if you meet with hostility, you can simply go on being a friend, and doing Christian work towards and around them.

The moment arrives

Though you can (and should!) pray for it, and though you can (and should!) ask questions to move towards it, you simply can't pick the way the conversation turns, or the moment a question is asked, that gives you the chance to share the gospel.

It may come in the form of an attack on an issue where Christ and your culture disagree. Sometimes it's a quiet comment from someone unexpected. It might be a question about what you think of science, or sex, or the future, or death. It could be something to do with you reacting differently, and surprisingly, to a problem or disappointment. It could be asked when you're tired, or when you're busy.

But when the moment comes, and you realise that you've just been presented with an opportunity to talk about Jesus Christ, you probably find your head is suddenly empty, except for the words:

WHAT DO I SAY?

I always find that I have the perfect answer... two hours after the question has been asked! But that's not much use—I need to have a sense of what to say in the moment when I have the chance to say it. And the key is, of course, that I proclaim Christ (2 Corinthians 4 v 5). That's my job—and over the years I've found that the following framework helps me to do just that. Here are two sets of three words that I remember...

Identity, Mission, Call

First, what do I need to say? *Identity. Mission. Call.* That's the gospel. Jesus' identity—who he is. Jesus' mission—why he came. Jesus' call—what he wants from us.

Second, how do I need to engage people as I talk about Identity, Mission and Call? *Understanding. Agreement. Impact.* To put it bluntly: *Do they get it? Do they agree with it? What are they doing about it?*

If I answer someone's question with a five-minute

monologue presenting the gospel, then that will be less effective than if I'm going through Identity, Mission and Call in a conversational way, one that stops to ask questions. I need to be listening as much as I am speaking. I want to be checking that the person I'm speaking to understands what it is I'm saying. But not only that—do they agree with it? And then, and this is absolutely crucial, I want to ask them to think about what they're going to do about it. Faith is not just knowing the content of the gospel, nor even agreeing with it; it is personally placing my trust in the person at the heart of it: the Lord Jesus.

Remembering these two sets of three words guards me against two mistakes. *Identity, Mission, Call* helps me remember the gospel, so that I explain it fully and clearly. *Understanding, Agreement, Impact* helps me remember that the guy or girl I'm speaking to is a person, not a project, so that I talk about Jesus relationally and lovingly.

In a sense, then, evangelism is a journey of gospel chatting. It's a dialogue, rather than a download. When my head is empty and I'm just thinking...

WHAT DO I SAY?

...I need to know what the gospel is—*Identity, Mission, Call*—and I need to remember how to communicate the gospel helpfully—*Understanding, Agreement, Impact*.

So the rest of this chapter lays out the *Identity, Mission, Call* framework of explaining the gospel. It's the kind of thing I'd want to say to someone who'd asked me what I believe or what Christianity is. If possible, I'd want to get the Bible open and show them where I was basing my explanation, so that they could see that it wasn't just my opinion or interpretation. But I'd also be wanting to move through the explanation conversationally, asking them questions, listening to their answers, seeing where they don't understand, or don't agree, or don't know what difference it can and should make to their lives.

Identity (Who Jesus is)

It can be very easy to see someone without seeing who they are.

I was invited to eat with a father and son in a very exclusive club in London—not a regular haunt for me. I found myself standing on the stairs of this restaurant waiting for my hosts. Opposite me, also waiting, was a man I vaguely recognised, but I thought nothing of it. So, as English people do, we gave each other a sheepish nod and waited awkwardly for five whole minutes in total silence.

Then a man came from round the corner and said: "Ah William, there you are. We're in the back dining room." I realised it was Prince William. I'd been with him for five minutes and we'd had nothing better to do than talk to each other... and I'd barely noticed him. I'd lost the opportunity for a once-in-a-lifetime conversation. I'd just seen a tall, young man with thinning blond hair. What I hadn't seen was that he was my future king.

Identity matters. And while missing Prince William's identity simply meant missing out on a conversation with him, when it comes to Jesus, it's much more important to realise who he is.

No ordinary guy

We need to start by realising that the only identity Jesus can't have is "ordinary guy". He was a man with amazing power—power over disease, over the weather, even over death.

So in Mark 8 v 27, at the turning point of Mark's Gospel, when Jesus asks his closest friends: "Who do people say I am?" none of the answers are: "Normal bloke":

> *"Some say John the Baptist; others say Elijah; and still others, one of the prophets." (v 28)*

Each of these was someone used by God to speak to people, to share God's truth in powerful ways. And everyone who's seen and heard Jesus knows that he's on a par with these great prophets of old.

But then Jesus asks a scorching question:

> *"But what about you?" he asked. "Who do you say I am?" (v 29)*

Verse 27 was a general information question, like asking: "Who won the last election?" But verse 29's question is personal, like asking: "Who did you vote for?" Jesus is saying: *You need to answer this question. You need to give your own personal response.*

And Peter gives his answer:

> *"You are the Messiah."*

Messiah is the Old Testament word for "anointed one"— the word the Bible uses for God's promised, chosen, all-powerful, eternal King. The Messiah—or the Christ, to use the Greek word—was the one whom God had promised, who would be human, but who would come with all God's authority, power and identity. He would be human, and he would be divine.

The question you can't duck

So the first question is: Who is Jesus? What is his identity? And the Gospels give us so many pieces of evidence to help us with that, because they show how Jesus teaches with authority, heals with power, stills storms with words, and claims to have the authority of God himself.

All of us have to answer this question. None of us can duck it.

> *"Who do you say I am?"*

Peter had seen the evidence, and he realised that Jesus is the Messiah, the Christ. God's King. God himself, walking in the world he made; the Creator living as a creature.

And then, strangely, Jesus "warned them not to tell anyone about him" (v 30).

Mission (Why Jesus came)

Why did Jesus want Peter and the others to keep quiet about his identity? Because Jesus knows it is not enough just to know who he is. We've got to know not just that he's the King, but what kind of King he is. Why did he leave heaven to come to earth?

> *He then began to teach them that the Son of Man must suffer many things and be rejected by the elders, the chief priests and the teachers of the law, and that he must be killed and after three days rise again. (v 31)*

Notice the word "must" occurs twice in that sentence. The word "must" means that something is necessary for something else to happen. Jesus is explaining his mission: *I have to be rejected; I have to die; I have to rise again, because you need me to do that.* Why do we need him to come and die and rise?

An answer to guilt

First, because we need forgiveness. We need an answer to guilt. Every human faces the difficult question: what do we do about our guilt when we are right to feel guilty?

Guilt is pretty unfashionable these days. But there is an appropriate guilt. It's how we ought to feel about the things that we have said and done that have hurt others, and have hurt the God who made them... about the times when we've ignored our Creator and just treated him as a footnote in our lives... about what the Bible calls sin.

You can explain away the feeling of guilt as social conditioning. You can try to erase it. You can find people who'll tell you that you don't need to feel it. But guilt is real. And feeling it is part of being a responsible human being. This is what the author Kingsley Amis said in an interview a few years ago, shortly before he died:

> *[To know] you can be forgiven your sins ... must be*
> *a wonderful thing. I carry my sins around with me.*
> *There's nobody there to forgive them.*

As Amis looked back on his own life, even by his own standards there were things that he'd done about which he was mighty ashamed.

And when Jesus says he must die, he is saying that he has come to take our guilt and its consequences; he has come to bring forgiveness for our sin. He came as the dying King. As he was executed, he prayed: "Father, forgive them" (Luke 23 v 34). That's what he was doing, hanging on a cross instead of sitting on his throne. He loves us so much that he came to take that punishment on himself; to die in our place; to pay for what we've done. As we look at the cross, we see God rescuing us by sacrificing himself. We see God bringing us into relationship with him so we can, as the seventeenth-century Westminster Confession puts it: "enjoy him for ever".

And this means that we can either pay for our own wrongdoing beyond death; or we can give it to Jesus in his death.

An answer to death

If we ask Jesus to take our guilt and give us forgiveness, then we know that we have a future. Jesus said his mission was to be the dying King, and then to be the risen King— "the Son of Man must ... after three days rise again" (Mark 8 v 31). Jesus came to provide an answer to guilt, and an answer to death. We need Jesus to rise again because we need him to give us hope in the face of death. Because he got through death himself, he can get me through. Because he lives beyond death himself, he can give me life beyond death too. I can have real hope.

The first funeral I performed of a relatively young man was of a 35-year-old called Stuart Spencer. He had a PhD, he was a professional musician... and he was dying of leukaemia. He asked me to lead his funeral. I was 27, and I visited him three days before he died, and I didn't really know what to say. So I suddenly blurted out:

"Stuart, what's it like to die?"

That's not the best question to ask someone who is facing death. But Stuart looked at me and he simply said:

"Rico, Christ is risen."

For all his achievements, that was all Stuart had as he faced his death. But it was all Stuart needed as he went through his death. Christ Jesus came to give people a future—a future with him.

Call (What it means for us)

Mark 8 v 34 is Jesus' description of what it will mean to follow him. It is one that no public-relations expert or marketing department would ever come up with:

> *Whoever wants to be my disciple must deny themselves*
> *and take up their cross and follow me.*

To become a Christian is neither convenient nor comfortable. It means no longer living for ourselves but for Jesus. I am not the ruler—he is. It means trusting and relying on Jesus, completely. I am not the rescuer—he is. Accepting this and living like it is what the Bible calls repenting.

Come and die

So following Jesus means change. We must refuse to downplay these words, to make them sound safer. It is a profoundly radical call to give our lives over to Jesus. It is a call to come and die.

The early 20th-century explorer Ernest Shackleton, when he was looking for people to go with him on his exploration to the Antarctic, reportedly placed an ad in a newspaper. It said simply:

> *Men wanted for hazardous journey. Low wages, bitter cold, long hours of complete darkness. Safe return doubtful. Honour and recognition in event of success.*

There is something of that in Jesus' call to each one of us. Following him will cost us a great deal. It will cost us in terms of comfort, careers, relationships and perhaps even life itself.

Come and live

But there's a crucial difference between Shackleton's call and Christ's call. It's the final outcome. Jesus has died to forgive sin, and has risen to secure our future with him. If we give our lives to him, it's not a suicidal gesture. In fact, it's the complete opposite:

> *Whoever wants to save their life will lose it, but whoever loses their life for me and for the gospel will save it.*
>
> *(v 35)*

If you give your life to Jesus, he will give you life. The One who calls us to give him everything is the One who has given everything for us, and who will give everything to us. As Jesus himself said:

> *Truly I tell you ... no one who has left home or brothers or sisters or mother or father or children or fields for me and the gospel will fail to receive a hundred times*

> *as much in this present age ... and in the age to come*
> *eternal life.*   *(10 v 29-30)*

Christ's call to follow him as our King is a call to come, and die... and live.

Honesty in evangelism

So, here is what I need to say if I am to evangelise.

Identity: Jesus is the Christ—a human, and God; our King.

Mission: Jesus came to die to take our punishment and remove our guilt so that we can be part of his eternal kingdom, now and beyond death, enjoying life with him for ever.

Call: Jesus calls us to follow him as our King. This is hard, but infinitely and eternally worth it.

Each aspect of the gospel requires us to cross the painline. Jesus is the Christ, the King—so you are not. Jesus is the dying, rising King—without him, you will pay for your sin and have no hope beyond death. Jesus calls us to follow him and deny ourselves—you will no longer be in charge of your life.

And so it's very tempting to leave some of it out! But if I am to witness honestly, I need to cover all three. In a courtroom, a witness is to tell the truth, the whole truth, and nothing but the truth—and Jesus tells his people to be his witnesses (Acts 1 v 8). I need to aim to tell someone enough for them to become a Christian; for them to turn to Jesus as their Ruler and trust him as their Rescuer. That may, of course, take several conversations; but that's got to be my aim.

This helps me know the direction I want to move a conversation in. If someone asks me about prayer, I want to be talking not so much about when I pray, or how it makes me feel, but who it is I'm praying to—the identity of Jesus. If someone asks me about how I became a Christian, I want to use that as a springboard to talk about how I came to understand Christ's mission.

By the way, it might be that as you've read this chapter, you've realised that you've never really come to Jesus and repented and believed—that you don't follow him as your King and trust him as your Rescuer. Well, wouldn't today be a great day to hear his call to come, and die, and live? What is stopping you from accepting him as your King and asking him to be your Saviour?

Evangelism is not about saying everything, or saying it eloquently. But it is about saying enough. *Identity. Mission. Call.* Do they understand? Do they agree? Has it impacted? If you've explained these things to someone, however hard you found it and however haltingly you said it, that's the gospel. You've preached Christ as he asks you to. The rest, as we saw in the last chapter, is up to God.

6. BE YOURSELF

I've often asked myself why it was that I got a Third (that's equivalent to about 2.1 GPA in the US) at university.

When I got my grade, I went to see my tutor, and I asked him: "Was I close to a 2:2?" and he said: "No, it was a very solid Third".

So I've often wondered why I didn't do as well as most students do. And I think that, apart from the fact that I was studying theology—and to a dyslexic, the English alphabet is challenging enough, let alone the Greek one—one of the reasons was that often I thought I'd understood a subject when in fact I hadn't. Time and again, I'd get an exam paper back, see the mark, look through it and realise I'd completely missed the main point.

And sadly, my inability to see the main point continued. For two years, I worked for a church as an "evangelist" before I realised what my job was. I'd always thought that being employed as an evangelist meant that my job was to evangelise. It sounds obvious. And then one day my understanding of what an evangelist should do was torpedoed by a single verse:

> *It was [Christ] who gave some to be apostles, some to be*
> *prophets, some to be evangelists, and some to be pastors*
> *and teachers, to prepare God's people for works of*
> *service, so that the body of Christ may be built up.*
>
> *(Ephesians 4 v 11, NIV84)*

Here, an evangelist is someone who prepares God's people for works of service—someone who not only talks to non-Christians about Jesus themselves, but who also encourages and equips other Christians to do the same, too. In other words, you don't need to be an "evangelist" to do evangelism. The job of people employed to be evangelists is not to take that responsibility away from other members of their church, but to help them to live out that responsibility as a joyful, though at times costly, privilege.

But I'm not an evangelist

This really helps us as we get to this part of the book. Reading this far means that you know what to expect as you talk about Jesus—hostility and hunger; and you know why you should talk about Jesus; and you know what to say about Jesus.

But... you're not an evangelist. When you think about doing evangelism, you immediately feel intimidated or terrified or unable (or all three). Why? Because you're thinking: *But I'm not like Billy Graham/John Chapman/ Helen Roseveare/Becky Manley Pippert/J John/my friend who seems to talk to Jesus naturally and compellingly with strangers on the bus. I'm just not like those people.*

And here's the great news. You don't need to be.

Instead of thinking of those "evangelists", think of the person who led you to Christ, or (if you've been a Christian longer than you can remember) the person who was most important in you understanding your faith. Maybe it was a parent, a sibling, a friend or a pastor. What qualities did they have, that person who reached you with the gospel?

I'm guessing you're thinking *integrity; sincerity; persistence; enthusiasm; courage; care.* The interesting thing about that list is that those are attainable qualities for all of us. With the help of God's Spirit, you can be that kind of person, the kind of person who leads others to faith.

I think one of the reasons we get spooked by the idea of evangelism is that the devil has played a cunning trick on the church. He's convinced us either that it's something that is not our job, or that it's something that should be our job but we can't do it. He whispers to us: *You're not an evangelist. You're not confident/outgoing/good at answering questions. You don't need to evangelise. You can't evangelise!*

So the key thing I want to say about you and your witness is this: be yourself.

Just be you

If you're going to take the gospel out to people, you've got to be yourself. After all, that's who God has made you to be:

> *You created my inmost being;*
>> *you knit me together in my mother's womb.*
> *I praise you because I am fearfully and wonderfully made;*
>> *your works are wonderful, I know that full well.*
>> *(Psalm 139 v 13-14)*

God knows who you are, and he knew what he was doing when he made you. He gave you your particular skills, temperament, intellect, fears, likes and dislikes. We are all different, and we are all wired to serve God in a unique way.

Sometimes, evangelistic books and training basically say: *Be more like him,* or: *Be more like her.* And people get discouraged, because they're not made that way.

But God could have made you to be a high-profile evangelist. He chose not to. He chose to make you to be you. And (as we saw in the last chapter) he put you exactly where you are. Maybe Billy Graham would be no good at witnessing to the others in your office. Perhaps Helen Roseveare's personality would mean she would be less effective than you at witnessing to the parents of your children's friends. God wants to harness what he has made you to be in order to reach a messed-up world with the unique combination of characteristics that you are.

I can't tell you how often I see the liberating effects of this. You don't have to be someone you're not: just the person God made you. But it also leaves us without excuses! You don't get a free pass out of evangelism because God didn't make you to be an evangelist.

So with that in mind, we can look in the New Testament and see different ways that different people seek to reach others with the gospel. (This is a helpful approach that I learned from a book called *Becoming a Contagious Christian,* by Bill Hybels and Mark Mittelberg.) Let's look at some of those people now—they are not mutually exclusive (you may fit more than one of them), but it's worth asking:

Which am I? Which one of these roles is right for me as I seek to reach others?

Peter

Peter was confrontational. Maybe you're someone for whom the confrontational approach is right. Peter's approach was: *Ready, Aim, Fire.*

So at Pentecost, when the Spirit has come on the first Christians, and others are wondering what on earth is going on, who is it who stands up? It's Peter. And what does he say?

> *Jesus of Nazareth was a man accredited by God to you by miracles, wonders and signs ... and you, with the help of wicked men, put him to death by nailing him to the cross ... Be assured of this: God has made this Jesus, whom you crucified, both Lord and Messiah.*
>
> *(Acts 2 v 22-23, 36)*

Peter gives it to them absolutely straight between the eyes. He says: *You killed Christ.* Now that is some people's style. They'll stand up and just tell you straight. Peter was certainly like that. He was just a natural at confronting people, and actually some people will never come to Christ until someone has really confronted them.

Now, every personality trait we have can be used for great good—for God; or, in our sinfulness, that same trait can end up being used for ill—to serve ourselves. So if you're a confrontational sort of person—a Peter—let me encourage you to use that gift for the gospel, by using it to give people the gospel. But also, let me encourage you to pray that you will have wisdom and sensitivity in the way that you use that style. Don't assume it's what everyone out there needs; don't assume that it's the only way that your fellow Christians should be sharing the gospel. But do use it, for God's glory, to share his Son with people.

Paul

Paul could confront people; but his general style was a more considered, intellectual approach. Remember Paul in Athens? He's invited to address the elite there, and he begins:

> *People of Athens! I see that in every way you are very religious. For as I walked around and looked carefully at your objects of worship, I even found an altar with this inscription:* TO AN UNKNOWN GOD. *So you are ignorant of the very thing you worship—and this is what I am going to proclaim to you.*   *(Acts 17 v 22-23)*

Paul's approach was thoughtful, connected, logical and reasoned. He presented the gospel clearly to people. He defined it and he defended it. His was the kind of make-up that could sit down and write (or dictate) the book of Romans, that great, complex explanation and defence of the gospel.

Maybe that logical, reasoned approach is where you're at. If that is the case, can I recommend that you get to grips with some good apologetics (that is, Bible-based answers to common questions about Christianity—you'll find some good books recommended on pages 119-120). Use the person God has made you to be in order to listen well, think well, and then reason well, pointing to Christ in a logical, considered way.

The ex-blind man

Third, maybe your approach is testimonial.

You're like the ex-blind man in John 9. He's healed by Jesus, and the Pharisees try to lead him into a debate about whether Jesus is a sinner. And he refuses! He accepts that he doesn't know everything, but he does know what has happened to him:

> *Whether he [Jesus] is a sinner or not, I don't know. One thing I do know. I was blind but now I see!*
>
> *(John 9 v 25)*

When the Pharisees try to get him into a debate, he points them back to his own experience, this time with a challenge:

> *I have told you already and you did not listen. Why do you want to hear it again? Do you want to become his disciples too?*　*(v 27)*

That last question crosses the painline, doesn't it?! He's met by insults (v 28), is accused of being "steeped in sin at birth", and is thrown out of his synagogue (v 34).

A lot of people won't respond to confrontation or argument—they're not wired that way. But they will be struck by an authentic change in someone's life and by someone speaking of that change.

Maybe that's where you're at. And if your testimony isn't very dramatic—if it's no competition for "I was blind but now I see", don't worry—perhaps the ordinariness of it connects better with people's ordinary lives.

So if you're someone who can tell a story, who can open up about your own life and background and experience, will you use that to point to Jesus? Will you humbly accept that you can't answer every question thrown at you (by the way, a great response to a question during a conversation about Jesus is: "I don't know, but I'll find out and get back to you")? Will you boldly seek to speak about your life in such a way that you're pointing to who Christ is, why he came and what it means to have him as your King?

So the question to you is: can you give your testimony? Here are three hooks for you to hang it on, if you can remember becoming a Christian:

1. What was I like before?
2. What did Christ do for me?
3. What difference does he make?

And then at the end of that you'd say: "Does that make sense? Do you understand what I'm saying about who Jesus is and what he offers?"

Maybe you grew up in a Christian home and you've always known Jesus as your Lord and Saviour. Well, here are some hooks for you:

1. Why is my faith significant for how I view my present and my future?
2. How did I grow in this relationship?
3. What do the cross and resurrection mean to me now?

And then again you can ask: "Does that make sense? Do you understand what I'm saying about who Jesus is and what he offers?"

It's well worth writing your testimony down, to make sure that you're using it as well as you can. You want to be sure that, when someone asks you about your story, you won't talk only about yourself, or about your church, or even about your faith, but you'll talk about Christ. You want someone to walk away after hearing your story having been struck by Jesus, not by you.

The woman at the well

In John 4, Jesus meets a woman at a well. She's had five husbands and is now living with a man she's not married to, so she's had a lot of bereavement, or heartbreak, or both. Jesus tells her all about herself; he tells her about who he is, and she is transformed as she meets him. So what does she do?

> The woman went back to the town and said to the people, "Come, see a man who told me everything I've ever done. Could this be the Messiah?" (John 4 v 28-29)

Come and see. And they do—the people "came out of the town and made their way towards him" (v 30).

Perhaps you're a great inviter. You're hospitable and friendly and you can get people enthused about trying something—a hobby or a trip or whatever. Well, will you use that gift to invite people to come and see Jesus? Will you say: "This is who I believe Jesus to be, and this is why he came and what it means, but look, come along to this event, this service, this course—come and see for yourself"? Could you think of events to organize yourself, perhaps in your own house, to invite some non-Christians and some Christians to, with the explicit invitation for people to come and find out more about Jesus? Could you simply invite people to look at the Bible with you, to see Jesus there (more on this in chapter seven)?

Who are you?

I don't know which of these types of people you are. But I'm betting you're one of them, or a mixture of some of them. And I know that you're fearfully and wonderfully made to be exactly that person—and that God wants to reach people through the person he knit you together to be.

So, which are you? A "confrontation person" like Peter? Or a considered person like Paul? Or a story-telling testimonial person like the ex-blind man? Or an inviter and bringer like the woman at the well?

God has wired you to tell others in a way that allows you to be yourself. Evangelism is not just for extroverts, brainboxes or full-timers. It is your job, and in the Lord's strength you can do it. Why not put this book down and ask the Lord to show you what kind of person you are, and then ask him to show you how he might use you, as the person you are, to reach out with the gospel to others?

Striving *together*

Alongside this call to be yourself must, however, go another call: to flee from individualism. All Christians are made differently, but we're also made to work together. As an individual Christian, you may be a foot or a finger or a follicle, but you are part of a body, the church, and it is as part of that body that you are most yourself, and most useful, as you contribute to and depend on the rest of your church.

One of the most forgotten, most crucial words of the Christian life is "together". Paul says in Philippians 1 v 27:

> *Stand firm in the one Spirit, striving together as one for the faith of the gospel.*

As part of Christ's body, you share his Spirit and you share his gospel—so stand together. And yet the question that so often undoes an enthusiastic young Christian is not: "Do you love Christ Jesus?" (they do) or: "Do you love telling people about Christ?" (they do) but: "Do you love Christ's church?"

We need our church, and our church needs us:

> *God has placed the parts in the body, every one of them, just as he wanted them to be.* (1 Corinthians 12 v 18)

We strive together for the faith of the gospel, and part of the way in which we strive for the gospel is in evangelism. We are to do evangelism together, as church; and yet so often the indispensability of the local church in evangelism is forgotten. John Stott brilliantly articulates the centrality of its role in evangelism in *Our Guilty Silence*:

> *The invisibility of God is a great problem. It was already a problem to God's people in Old Testament days. Their pagan neighbours would taunt them,*

saying, "Where now is your god?" Their gods were visible and tangible, but Israel's God was neither. Today in our scientific culture young people are taught not to believe in anything which is not open to empirical investigation. How then has God solved the problem of his own invisibility? The first answer is of course "in Christ". Jesus Christ is the visible image of the invisible God. John 1 v 18: "No one has ever seen God, but God the only Son has made him known." "That's wonderful," people say, "but it was 2,000 years ago. Is there no way by which the invisible God makes himself visible today?" There is. We return to 1 John 4 v 12: "No-one has ever seen God." It is precisely the same introductory statement. But instead of continuing with reference to the Son of God, it continues: "if we love one another, God dwells in us." In other words, the invisible God, who once made himself visible in Christ, now makes himself visible in Christians, if we love one another. It is a breathtaking claim. The local church cannot evangelise, proclaiming the gospel of love, if it is not itself a community of love.

So it's not only the individual Christian believer who is to let their light shine, a narrow beam of torchlight in the word; each local church is to be a lighthouse: a great, wide beam of gospel light, illuminating the surrounding darkness.

If we are to stand firm in one Spirit, striving together as one for the faith of the gospel, we must not see our local church as just our campaign headquarters, from which we hear the gospel and go; and neither is it just our field hospital, where we return to be patched up. It is those things; but it is so much more. It is a loving community of Christian brothers and sisters, and by being this, it gives credibility to the gospel. Indeed, it is God's intended medium for his message. There is a sense in which witnessing to Christ can only happen if it is happening corporately—together.

So be yourself, and feel free to be yourself. In evangelism, use the character and gifts God has deliberately given you. But don't feel obliged to do it all by yourself. Use your character and gifts as part of the church in which God has deliberately placed you. Shine a gospel light in your office and in your local coffee shop; join it with the beams of others as you meet midweek in ways that include witnessing; and let it be part of the great lighthouse for your community that your church must be. As Jesus himself put it:

> *By this everyone will know that you are my disciples, if you love one another.* *(John 13 v 35)*

7. GETTING STARTED (OR RE-STARTED)

The content of Christian witness never changes. But the context of our witness does. And our culture changes fast, especially when it comes to how it views Christianity. That means that often we've just worked out how we can witness effectively when things move on, and we have to work it out all over again.

So here is a very basic little summary of what's happened culturally in the last 70 years in the UK. Usually, in cultural terms, the UK is a decade or two behind the US; but in spiritual terms, culturally, I think that the US is, in most areas and in most ways, a couple of decades behind the UK. In that sense, the church's experience east of the Atlantic has much to teach, warn and counsel the church in North America. But when it comes to Great Britain, here's what's happened over my lifetime...

1954

GOD

SIN

When the American evangelist Billy Graham came to the UK for the first time in 1954, he packed out stadiums night after night. He preached the cross, and thousands put their faith in Christ. The basics were already in place—a lot of people believed in a Creator God, and in the notion of sin, and in the truth that Jesus is God's Son. Billy Graham put that all together and explained the cross, and people repented and believed. When I was at university in the 1980s, a lot of the Christians my age were the children of people who had come to Christ at Billy Graham missions.

1994

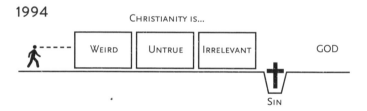

By the time I joined the staff at All Souls Langham Place in central London in 1994, the culture was hardening against Christianity. It was proving harder to get people to come to a guest service or hear a visiting evangelist. There were blocks in the way of people coming to faith—objections to Christianity that had to be dealt with and removed before the gospel could gain a hearing. Now, those blocks varied from place to place and person to person, but in London over and over again I came across the same three:

1. Christians are weird.
2. Christianity is untrue.
3. Christianity is irrelevant.

(Sometimes, and increasingly, people added a fourth: Christianity is intolerant.) So the challenge was to remove those obstacles. How did you do that? People needed to meet Christians; needed to see changed lives and love for others; and needed to hear answers to their intellectual issues. So Christians would meet people in their workplace or wherever, and after a while trust would build; they'd invite their colleague to a guest service, or an evangelistic course, and that person would be ready and willing to give the gospel a hearing. You removed the blocks in the road, and they walked along it.

TODAY

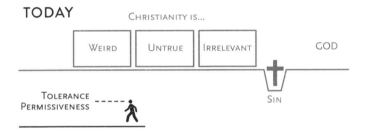

Today, just over twenty years later, people are on a totally different road. John Stott said, not long before he died, that our culture is defined by tolerance and permissiveness. Culturally, we're such a long way from biblical Christianity that people don't object to faith having engaged with it; they simply dismiss it. Jesus simply isn't on the agenda; he isn't even an option to be considered. People hardly ever think about why they don't agree with your beliefs; and if they ever do, they put it in the "It's fine for you, but it's not for me" box in their head. The culture is teaching people not to consider Christianity even when life goes wrong, or when there seems no point to anything, or when a loved one dies.

Evangelism for our time and place

What does this mean for our gospel proclamation? How can we witness effectively in the time and place God has placed us in? I think it means two things.

First, witnessing takes time and effort. The days when you could go from zero to the gospel in a single conversation are not the norm—keep praying for it, but don't be discouraged by it not happening. It's very rare for someone to meet a Christian, come to a guest service the next month, and then sign up for a *Christianity Explored*-type course. Research suggests that when people put their faith in Christ, on average it's taken two years from the point when they came into meaningful contact with a Christian who witnessed to them—and that time period is growing. Witnessing is a long-term commitment to invest in a relationship, to pray tirelessly, and to speak the gospel over and over again, patiently and persistently. It is a journey of gospel conversations. It really does take effort.

I can promise you that if you put into practice what's in this book, you will get hit. I can't promise you that you'll see very much fruit very quickly. When people start further back, they have a greater distance to travel.

Second, it takes *you*. It's harder and harder to take people to hear the Bible taught; you need to take the Bible to them. People who would never consider stepping into a church will feel far less threatened reading and talking about the Bible with a friend.

I think one of the most exciting and necessary developments in evangelism in the last decade or so in the UK has been the increased emphasis on evangelistic one-to-one Bible reading, where a Christian simply sits down with a non-Christian friend (or a few friends, though then it ought to be called one-to-several) and looks at the Bible with them. There is no silver bullet in evangelism; nothing erases the painline, and only God can open blind eyes. But one-to-one evangelism is nevertheless reaping a harvest. We've seen this in the huge fruit that has come from the use among students of *Uncover Luke*, part of which is a six-session set of evangelistic studies written by Becky Manley Pippert for Christians to use with small groups and individual non-Christians (Becky's material has now been re-published as *Uncovering the Life of Jesus*).

Why is one-to-one evangelism so key? Because it takes account of the truths that evangelism takes time, and evangelism takes friendship. The great benefit is that it enables us to meet people where they are at (both geographically and spiritually), rather than expecting them to come to where we are. When you read the Bible as a pair, it's a format that helps understanding; they can ask questions, clarify things, and so on. It's a great way to talk about the meaning for their own life; and a great way to show what it means for yours. It requires trust. Your friends won't open the Bible with Rico-the-pastor, and why should they—they don't know me, they don't trust me. But they do know you—they'll open up to you. And it's flexible: it can happen at a time and in a place that's convenient and non-threatening.

Of course, it can also—for the Christian—seem slightly intimidating and demanding. You're no longer saying: *Come and listen to an expert at my church.* You're saying: *Sit and chat about the Bible with me.* And you're no longer simply inviting friends to a carol service, a curry-with-a-gospel-talk or whatever else it is that your church is putting on; you're needing to commit your time and energy, as well as risk being vulnerable.

But remember, this is why God, in his sovereignty, has put you where you are. His grace is sufficient for you; his power is enough to open anyone's eyes. We aren't all called to be Bible teachers; but we can all be Bible sharers. And in the culture we live in, we will need to be.

How to do it

How do you know what to do, or what to say? Well, make use of resources (there are some suggestions on pages 119-120). Or take a passage; ask some questions about it that explore it; work out how you'd explain it to a friend; then think hard about how it encourages you to love Jesus. Then do the exploring, share the explanation, and think about the encouragement with your friend.

One approach is to sit down with someone, tell them the Bible section you're going to look at, and suggest that once you've both read it, you could both share your answers to three questions:

1. What strikes me here?
2. What don't I understand here? And what's my best guess at the answer?

3. What is this passage encouraging me to change in my attitudes or my actions?

So, once you've read the passage, you can say: *Would you like to tell me what struck you, or would you like me to go first?* (Almost always, they pick you to go first!) So you then explain, very simply and honestly, what struck you. Then they tell you what struck them, and you chat about it. You share the questions you have, and your applications (which can, of course, be different). It's a great way to make looking at the Bible a conversation, teasing out misunderstandings in a non-confrontational way and chatting through them, and modelling to your friend how to read a Bible passage and allow it to change you.

So think of a friend or family member you could go to and say: "Would you like to read the Bible with me?" Or maybe there are three or four of you that could get together. Think beforehand of where you could go to look at it with them—somewhere comfortable and non-threatening for both of you. I will often go with the passage on two bits of paper—I won't go with the Bible if we're in a public place—because then I can give my friend the bit of paper to look at and, once we've looked at it, they can take it away with them.

How to get started

Preachers love to use words that start with the same letter for titles—so here's what you need to get started: four things all beginning with "C":

1. Character

Character is simply this: are you a Christian who repents and believes? Are you repenting of the idols that convince you not to risk witnessing? Are you someone who regularly turns away from their sin and back to Jesus as Lord? Do you have a real sense that the gospel is for you—that Jesus' death and resurrection really is your only answer to guilt and to death? I've found that people who are serious about rooting out their idolatry, and who are increasingly in love with the Lord Jesus, are also people who are passionate about witnessing.

2. Conviction

Are you convinced of God's sovereignty? His grace? His power? As we saw in chapter four, you need to have those three things in place. That's the first conviction: *God has put me here; God loves me in Christ; and as I preach Christ, God opens blind eyes.*

The second is this: *This is my job. It's not just the pastor's job; it's not just the experts' job. I may not be a Bible teacher, but I am to be a Bible sharer. I'm to be myself, but I am to be a witness.*

3. Competence

The first time I read the Bible with someone was in my early twenties. There was a guy in my rugby team called Andy, and he walked up to me at training and said: "My brother was killed in a farm accident in the summer". I said something brilliant like: "Oh, man". He said: "My brother was a Christian". Trying to top the brilliance of my first reply, I said: "He was a Christian?" "Yes," he said: "It's really made me think." And then, before I really knew what I was saying, I said: "Do you want to look at the Bible with me?" And he said: "Yes".

So I knocked on the door of his flat, and he opened the door and I went in. Someone had told me Isaiah 53 was a good passage. So I got out Isaiah 53 and I'd scribbled down some questions. I was just so nervous that I started sweating everywhere.

Andy said: "You're sweating all over the Bible!" I said: "I'm fine, I'm fine! I've got some questions for you, Andy." I read Isaiah 53 and then asked him four questions. He was a typical rugby guy, and he just answered: "Yes... no... no... yes." It was over in two minutes. I prayed, and then said: "Do you want to meet again next week?" And Andy said: "Yes. But are you going to sweat as much next time?"

That was over twenty years ago. I'm a bit better at it now—and I don't sweat so much. And I have learned that it is all about practice—it doesn't make you perfect, but it does make you better.

So, practise! If you read chapter five and thought: *I don't think I can remember what to say about Identity, Mission, Call...* if you read the previous chapter and thought: *I'm really not clear on what type of person I am...* if you read this chapter about opening the Bible one to one and thought: *I wouldn't know where to start with that...* practise! If these things are really excuses for not crossing the painline and not getting hit, then you'll keep making them. If they're just weaknesses that come from inexperience, then you'll ask someone at church to read the Bible with you so you can learn how to do it. You'll ask a Christian friend to help you explain your faith more clearly. You'll write down your testimony and memorise it.

You don't need to be good at witnessing; you simply need to be faithful in doing it. If you feel completely inadequate, get on your knees to pray about it, rather than ducking out of it.

4. Courage

It isn't easy. You're risking rejection and mockery. You're crossing the painline. You need to ask God to give you the courage to say: "Would you like to look at the Bible with me?" Just ask. Just get started. Just remember the wonder of the gospel, the truth of the gospel and the power of the gospel. "Would you like to look at the Bible with me?" There'll be someone you could ask today.

8. TWO THINGS
TO DO

When I left school, I became a youth worker at Shrewsbury House, Liverpool—a youth club in Everton. In the mid-1980s, Liverpool was a place of real political unrest, and for all the joy of being surrounded by Scouse humour, I was shocked by the poverty I saw. I remember being told that over the years, seven young mums had jumped off the tower block outside our hostel's window.

Two things struck me: the people who wanted to change things were powerless to do so, and whoever did have any real power seemed to have little inclination to listen or care. It made me long for someone with both compassion and authority—with the desire to help, and the power to do so.

There are lots of people who have authority, but not much compassion. And there are many with compassion, but little power to effect change. One of the most wonderful things about the Bible is that as we read of Jesus, we meet a man who had more of both than anyone who has ever lived, and who never compromised on either—a man of complete authority and overwhelming compassion.

For instance, take these verses. They're a summary of the whole of Matthew's Gospel from chapter 5 – 9:

> *Jesus went through all the towns and villages, teaching in their synagogues, proclaiming the good news of the kingdom and healing every disease and illness. When he saw the crowds, he had compassion on them...*
>
> *(Matthew 9 v 35-36)*

The two key words there are "kingdom" and "compassion". Kingdoms have kings, and here is the King telling people and showing people his authority. In the previous chapters, he's shown that he's a ruler with authority over ethics, over disease, over blindness, over nature and over death itself. These are glimpses of his unique authority and they are glimpses of his glorious kingdom. Here is the King, announcing that his kingdom has arrived, and inviting people in.

Compassion is what Jesus felt as he looked at the crowds who gathered to see him. The Greek word translated "compassion" literally means that his bowels moved within him—he had a gut reaction to these crowds. Have you ever seen someone in desperate trouble or poverty or grief, and you feel your stomach churn as you literally ache for them and their plight? That's how Jesus felt about the crowds around him. They were not annoying to him, or intimidating to him. They aroused his compassion.

Why? Because:

> *They were harassed and helpless, like sheep without a shepherd.*
>
> *(v 36)*

That's what Jesus saw. He saw people who were in need of a leader, a shepherd, someone to guide them and protect them. Without that guidance and protection, they were anxious, rudderless, unfulfilled, stressed, and with no answer to the death they were all wandering towards. They needed a shepherd to guide them through life and protect them through death. They needed him. John Calvin, the great sixteenth-century Reformer, said of these verses:

> *The whole life of man until he is converted to Christ is a ruinous labyrinth of wanderings, harassed and helpless.*

Jesus' compassion is wonderful, and challenging. It's wonderful because it is the compassion that brought him to earth to announce his kingdom, and that sent him to the cross to open the way into his kingdom, and that will see him return one day to finally establish his kingdom. But it's also challenging, because the question for us is: "How do *we* see those around us, and how do *we* react to those around us?" Do we see their success, their possessions, their confidence, all the things that are impressive? Or do we see that, deep down, they are harassed and helpless, wandering in a ruinous labyrinth that exits only into death? And do we react to people with compassion that will give everything and risk everything to bring them to their Shepherd?

I've already mentioned Henry Martyn. He wrote:

> *Let me never fancy that I have zeal until my heart overflows with love to every human being.*

How I need to pray for that kind of love: a Christ-like compassion! The truths and encouragements of the Bible that we've looked at in this book will never do anything for any of us unless we are praying that we would see people as Jesus did: with compassion, because they are without a shepherd, harassed and helpless.

Ask the Lord

And we're right to pray. Jesus tells us to!

> Then he said to his disciples, "The harvest is plentiful but the workers are few. Ask the Lord of the harvest, therefore, to send out workers into his harvest field." (v 37-38)

Jesus saw these people in two ways: as sheep without a shepherd, and also as a plentiful harvest—a waving field of corn waiting to be reaped. There are all these thousands of people who need to be told about the kingdom and pointed to the Shepherd, and there are so few workers. There's no one to do the harvesting. And so he tells his friends to pray—that activity that often seems so small and inconsequential, and yet changes the world and transforms eternal destinies. As Simon Barrington-Ward, the former bishop of Coventry, memorably puts it:

> Prayer is that apparently useless activity, without which all activities are useless.

So whatever else you do as a result of reading this book, I hope you'll pray; I hope you'll ask. Pray to God to raise up workers for every corner of the harvest field. Compassion will see us on our knees, asking God to make sure that there are people bringing the harvest in. There is great urgency—there are sheep without a shepherd, unprotected from death—let's pray. There is great opportunity—there is a harvest waiting to be brought in, if only there are harvesters to do it—let's pray.

Go, proclaim

And I hope that, having prayed, we'll be obedient. I hope we'll be willing in some way to be the answer to our own prayer. In the original Bible text, there is no chapter division between what Jesus says:

> *Ask the Lord of the harvest, therefore, to send out workers into his harvest field.* *(v 38)*

... and what he then does:

> *Jesus called his twelve disciples to him and gave them authority to drive out impure spirits and to heal every disease and illness. ... [He told them] "Proclaim this message: 'The kingdom of heaven has come near.' Heal those who are ill, raise the dead, cleanse those who have leprosy, drive out demons. Freely you have received; freely give."* *(10 v 1, 7-8)*

Jesus says: *See people as they really are. Love people with compassion. Pray for people to tell them the gospel. Then go and do it.* He says to these followers: *Go out and change the world.* What a responsibility!

And at the end of this Gospel, Jesus calls all of us to do the same—to go: "Go and make disciples" (Matthew 28 v 19). It's important to say that the mission Jesus gives in

Matthew 28 is not quite the same as the one in Matthew 10. These disciples in chapter 10 were given authority to give glimpses of the kingdom—healing the sick, raising the dead, cleansing the leper and driving out demons. In chapter 28, Jesus did not give that authority permanently to his people. These disciples in Matthew 10 were told to "go ... to the lost sheep of Israel", and only to them (10 v 6). In Matthew 28, Jesus told his followers for the rest of history to "make disciples of all nations"—we have a wider horizon!

So the command to us is not identical in detail, but it is the same in essence: first, to pray for workers; and second, to go out and be those workers. We must pray before we go; and we must go and proclaim. Neither is an optional extra in the Christian life.

Where is your harvest field? It's your workplace, your family, your street, your sports club, your social group. Who knows what harvest is there? Who knows how many people have been praying for years for the people you will sit next to or speak to today? This is the corner of the global harvest field where Jesus says to you: *Go, proclaim the kingdom.* And as you go, see what encouragement there is here. First, there is a Lord of the harvest, and it's not you. This does not depend on you—it is the Lord's work, and he invites you to have the privilege of being part of it. And second, Jesus tells us the harvest is plentiful. So we can expect real hunger in the corner of the harvest field in which we've been placed, even if it's not immediately obvious to us.

Available?

And so the question we need to finish with is: *Are you available for work?* It's the greatest work there is, because it's work that is eternally significant. In many ways it's the hardest work there is, because it will sometimes meet with hostility, and so there is always a painline to be crossed. In every way it's the most exciting work there is, because as you take a risk to talk about the King of the kingdom, the divine Shepherd of his flock, you will discover hunger for the gospel in surprising and thrilling places.

The great news is that any Christian can do this job, because Jesus can work through anyone. After all, in Matthew 10 the twelve people he sent out on mission included Simon Peter, who would be an impetuous deserter; Thomas, the doubter; Matthew, the tax collector, who was a traitor to his people; Simon the Zealot, who was obsessed with freedom fighting; and Judas Iscariot, who would betray Christ. What a group! Is there anything positive to say about them? One thing: they were available. They weren't great, but they were ready to go. They didn't know everything, but they knew enough to tell people about the Man who has complete authority and overwhelming compassion: the One who is Ruler and Rescuer.

Are you available? As you put down this book, will you pray, and ask the Lord to make you willing, give you words, help you make opportunities, enable you to take opportunities, and then empower you to proclaim that Jesus Christ is Lord?

If you're like me, you'll never find evangelism easy. You'll always find it hard to take the risk, and get over the painline. Let's remember:

- *There will be hunger as well as hostility.*
- *Jesus Christ is glorious; the new creation is wonderful; death and hell are real.*
- *God is sovereign; he is gracious; and he is powerful.*

Let's pray. And then let's go. Seeing people come to Christ is such an indescribable joy.

Are you available?

USEFUL RESOURCES

Books on evangelism:
Know and Tell the Gospel (John Chapman)
Out of the Saltshaker and into the World (Rebecca Manley Pippert)
Evangelism and the Sovereignty of God (J.I. Packer)
The Gospel and Personal Evangelism (Mark Dever)
Questioning Evangelism (Randy Newman)
Tactics (Greg Koukl)
Becoming a Contagious Christian (Bill Hybels & Mark Mittelberg)

Books on the gospel:
Scandalous (D.A. Carson)
Real Life Jesus (Mike Cain)
What is the Gospel? (Greg Gilbert)
The Cross of Christ (John Stott)
Christ the King (Tim Keller)

Books on apologetics (answering common objections to the Christian faith):
The Reason for God (Tim Keller)
If You Could Ask God One Question (Paul Williams & Barry Cooper)

Tricky (Michael Dormandy & Carl Laferton)
On suffering: *If I were God... I'd end all the pain*
(John Dickson)
On homosexuality: *Is God Anti-Gay?* (Sam Allberry)
On the Bible's trustworthiness: *Gospel Truth* (Paul Barnett);
Can I Really Trust the Bible? (Barry Cooper)
On science: *Can Science Explain Every Thing?; God's Undertaker* (John Lennox)

Books/Resources to give away:
One Life. What's it all About? (Rico Tice & Barry Cooper)
A Fresh Start (John Chapman)
Original Jesus (Carl Laferton)
321: The Story of God, the World and You (Glen Scrivener)
Mere Christianity (C.S. Lewis)
For those with serious/terminal illness: *Hope Beyond Cure* (David McDonald)

Tracts:
The Choice We All Face (Phillip Jensen and Tony Payne)
Jesus: Who, Why, So What? (Barry Cooper & Carl Laferton)
The Real Jesus (Rico Tice & Barry Cooper)

One-to-One resources:
Uncovering the Life of Jesus (Rebecca Manley Pippert)
You, Me and the Bible (Tony Payne)
Uncover John (UCCF)
The Word One to One (Richard Borgonon)
On how to do one-to-one reading (with Christians and non-Christians): *One-to-One Bible Reading* (David Helm)

THANK YOU...

... to my co-author, Carl, for inspiring the project and helping with the writing of it; and to my publisher, The Good Book Company, for constant support over 20 years.

... to Grace McDowell, my PA at All Souls, for selfless service, patience and efficiency.

... to the All Souls church family, for being the "laboratory" in which all this has been worked out; for honest and perceptive feedback on this book; and for the gift of the sabbatical that gave me space and time to think these things through.

... to Eddie and Maureen Green, for babysitting while Lucy and I worked on the manuscript.

... to my older brother George, for leading me to Christ and for contstant care and protection; and to Scarlett, ever gracious.

... to my sister and brother in law, Camilla and Andrew, for such wholehearted support.

... to Christopher and Carolyn Ash, with thanks for faithfulness to my brother and me in the early years.

... to Hugh and Clare Palmer, for selfless service and leadership at All Souls; and to all my colleagues at All Souls and at Christianity Explored Ministries, for so much support and feedback in so many ways.

CHRISTIANITY|EXPLORED

Christianity Explored gives you time to think about the big questions of life and to consider the life of the person at the heart of the Christian faith - Jesus Christ.

- *Seven week journey through the Gospel of Mark*
- *Stunning DVD presented by Rico Tice in locations around the UK*
- *Comprehensive leader's guide so anyone can run the course*

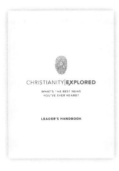

Christianity Explored is wonderfully Christocentric, it is entirely gospel focused, it is manageable material and it has been well crafted.

ALISTAIR BEGG, SENIOR PASTOR, PARKSIDE CHURCH, OHIO

For guests:
www.christianityexplored.org

For leaders:
www.ceministries.org

One life: What's it all about?

Rico Tice and Barry Cooper

This jargon-free, straight-talking book explores life's big questions and the life of the person at the heart of the Christian faith—Jesus Christ. Great as a companion to the Christianity Explored course, or for anyone wanting to explore what life's all about.

If you could ask God one question

Paul Williams and Barry Cooper

If you could ask God one question, and you knew that he would answer, what would it be? Every participant on Christianity Explored thinks about this question in week 1 of the course, and the most common responses have been brought together in this engaging, humorous and Christ-centred book.

Jesus, who why so what?

Barry Cooper and Carl Laferton

A compelling, straightforward booklet which uses five dynamic pictures to explain the gospel—who Jesus is, why he came, and what that means for each one of us. Perfect for churches to give away at guest events, and for Christians to give to interested friends.

LIFE|EXPLORED

Over seven sessions, *Life Explored* helps people uncover what they're really living for, and shows how, in Christ, God meets our deepest desire for happiness. It's perfect for anyone looking for answers to life's big questions.

Life Explored can be enjoyed one-to-one, in larger groups, in churches, or in homes.

It is a pleasure to recommend Life Explored. This is one of the best of the rising number of evangelistic tools addressing men and women in the twenty-first century.

D. A. CARSON

www.life.explo.red

DISCIPLESHIP|EXPLORED

Discipleship Explored has been developed to help people understand what's involved in living as a disciple of Jesus. Documentary-style films shot around the world take us on an eight-session journey through Paul's letter to the Philippians to discover the best love we could ever know.

It is great for new Christians, or anyone wanting to re-cap the basics or study the book of Philippians.

CHRISTIANITY
EXPLORED
MINISTRIES

www.discipleship.explo.red

'ENGAGING WITH' SERIES

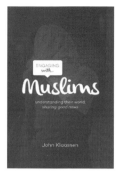

Engaging with Muslims
John Klaassen

Many Christians in the West are fearful of engaging in conversation with Muslims, believing that they will be hostile to Christian beliefs and conversations about the Bible. This short book will help you understand more about the variety of Muslims there are living in the West, and to reach out to them with the good news of the gospel.

Engaging with atheists
David Robertson

David Robertson shares his wide experience of debating the Christian faith with atheists to enable you to be equipped to deal with the questions and issues they have, and how best to engage with them and lead them towards Christ.

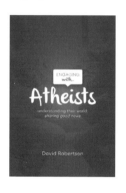

Engaging with Hindus
Robin Thomson

Hindus are the third largest faith in the world, and yet many Christians know very little about their beliefs and lifestyle. Robin Thomson has spent years living amongst Hindus and offers his wisdom on how to encourage friendly engagement, rather than argument, as you share your faith.

www.thegoodbook.com/engaging

UNCOVERING THE LIFE OF JESUS

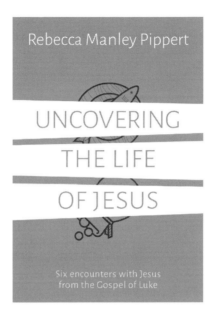

Rebecca Manley Pippert

UNCOVERING
THE LIFE
OF JESUS

Six encounters with Jesus
from the Gospel of Luke

Uncovering the Life of Jesus

Rebecca Manley Pippert

Becky Pippert's experience in evangelism and understanding of the
mindset of non-Christians shines through on each page of these
six Bible studies, written for a Christian to use one to one, or with a
group of interested non-Christians, helping them to meet the real
Jesus. It can be used by any Christian: no previous experience or
expertise necessary!

www.thegoodbook.com/ulj

thegoodbook
COMPANY

Thanks for reading this book. We hope you enjoyed it, and found it helpful.

Most people want to find answers to the big questions of life: Who are we? Why are we here? How should we live? But for many valid reasons we are often unable to find the time or the right space to think positively and carefully about them.

Perhaps you have questions that you need an answer for. Perhaps you have met Christians who have seemed unsympathetic or incomprehensible. Or maybe you are someone who has grown up believing, but need help to make things a little clearer.

At The Good Book Company, we're passionate about producing materials that help people of all ages and stages understand the heart of the Christian message, which is found in the pages of the Bible.

Whoever you are, and wherever you are at when it comes to these big questions, we hope we can help. As a publisher we want to help you look at the good book that is the Bible because we're convinced that as we meet the person who stands at its heart—Jesus Christ—we find the clearest answers to our biggest questions.

Visit our website to discover the range of books, videos and other resources we produce, or visit our partner site www.christianityexplored.org for a clear explanation of who Jesus is and why he came.

Thanks again for reading,

Your friends at The Good Book Company

thegoodbook.com | thegoodbook.co.uk
thegoodbook.com.au | thegoodbook.co.nz | thegoodbook.co.in

WWW.CHRISTIANITYEXPLORED.ORG

Our partner site is a great place to explore the Christian faith, with powerful testimonies and answers to difficult questions.